ON A STICK!

·········{ 80 Party-Perfect Recipes *by* Matt Armendariz }·········

Dedicated to my parents, Ben and Helen Armendariz, and Adam,
for nurturing me and giving me the love, strength, and space to dream,
to play, to explore and follow my heart.
I love you.

Library of Congress Cataloging in Publication Number: 2010940145

ISBN: 978-1-59474-489-1

Printed in China

Typeset in ITC Serif Gothic, Rockwell, Sabon, and Eureka Sans

Designed by Jenny Kraemer and Katie Hatz
Production management by John J. McGurk
Photography by Matt Armendariz
mattbites.com

10 9 8 7 6 5 4 3 2 1

Quirk Books
215 Church Street
Philadelphia, PA 19106
www.quirkbooks.com

Contents

Introduction

The results are in, thanks to teams of researchers and scientists: Foods on a stick just taste better.

OK, I made that up. Of course there's no scientific study to prove that serving foods on sticks makes them more enjoyable and more lip-smacking than they otherwise would be. But you know what? I don't think we need research. Ask anyone who's ever snacked at a state fair or nibbled on street cuisine in some exotic, faraway place. They'll all tell you the same thing: Eating food on a stick is fun, festive, and just plain delicious.

And it's nothing new. We've been cooking food on a stick since the dawn of history. Long before the invention of kitchen utensils, people were grilling over an open fire, using branches to warm and roast food. This cooking method appears in the writings of the ancient Greeks, and virtually all cultures since have offered their own version of food on a stick. Satay, an Asian variety, usually features pork or chicken, while kebabs, which originated in the Middle East, can be made with anything from lamb to beef. Greek cooking has souvlaki, and the French use a technique known as *en brochette,* in which food is skewered and usually grilled.

Let's fast-forward to modern times, shall we? Thanks to the ingenuity of creative cooks, whimsical chefs, and festival owners, we've now entered the golden age of food on a stick. If you don't believe me, pay a visit to the Minnesota State Fair, where you'll find anything and everything served on a

{pork chop on a stick!}

{pizza on a stick!}

stick. Deep-fried Coca Cola munched off a stick? Yep, it's been done. Mac 'n' cheese that's eaten vertically? That exists, too. Highbrow to lowbrow, scrumptious to silly, state fairs are pushing the limits of what can be served on a stick. (If by chance you feel the need to investigate these culinary innovations on your own, give me a call. I just might join you.)

Silliness aside, foods on sticks are perfect for upping the enjoyment ante of all sorts of occasions. Sure, they're practical, but I like to think of them as being infused with an automatic fun factor. If you don't believe me, try this experiment: Cut up some fresh fruit; serve a bunch of pieces in a bowl and, next to them, a few that have been skewered. No contest—people will go for the sticks every time. Maybe it's because of convenience or maybe it's just a joy to eat, who knows? Food on a stick is a natural for all sorts of occasions, and especially for dining al fresco. You can eliminate the extra plates and toss out the cutlery, too!

When it comes to food, I believe variety is the spice of life. So in this book I've made sure to include something for everyone, from health-conscious vegetarians to carnivores of the he-man grilling club (I'm a charter member!). And if you came here looking for those over-the-top state fair behemoths, well, I aim to please. I just had to find room for a few of my favorite indulgences. (But I implore you: For Pete's sake, consume those deep-fried, chocolate and/or bacon-laden treats in moderation, won't you?) I'm a fan of all types of cuisine, and I believe that eating food in its most natural state, free from processing and additives, is the way to go. Fortunately, it's extra easy to get more than your daily dose of fresh fruits and veggies when they're offered as tempting stick-worthy hors d'oeuvres.

{ deep-fried Snickers on a stick! }

I truly love making stick foods for guests, both for the sheer convenience of serving them and for the delight everyone gets from eating them. To help with your own party-perfect presentations, I've shared some of my favorite entertaining techniques and tips. And when assembling the menu for your skewered-food soiree, be sure to choose both savory and sweet recipes from the many in this book. For example, with their shared Spanish roots, Pinchos de Gambas (page 84) and Red and White Sangria Pops (page 170) make a perfect pair. Or try an all-vegetarian Italian spread: Panzanella (page 83) alongside Deep-Fried Ravioli (page 59) or Suppli (page 108). And don't forget to indulge your sweet tooth—and inner child—by digging into decadent desserts and state-fair favorites, from Cake Pops (page 122) and Caramel Popcorn Balls (page 129) to Deep-Fried Candy Bars (page 142) and Tornado Potato Sticks (page 115).

At the heart of serving food on a stick is experimentation and thinking off the plate, so don't be afraid to invent a few recipes of your own. There's something about skewered food that brings smiles to people's faces. It's portable, it's hand-hold-able, and it's just plain fun.

Sticks & Skewers

Skewer it, stab it, stick it! All sorts of wonderful sticks, skewers, and aromatic herbs can be used to make food that's fun to eat without silverware.

{Sugarcane}
This organic material makes a sturdy woody skewer that's perfect for hoisting heavier foods and bringing out the wonderful flavor of meat and seafood. It imparts a sugary taste and is especially good with grilled, smoky fare.

{Candy Sticks}
These paper products are best suited for sweets and single-skewered items, like candy, cake pops, and s'mores.

{Rosemary Skewers}
The woody older branches of this aromatic plant make wonderful skewers by infusing meat and fish with herbal flavor. Soak them first, and use a stronger skewer to poke holes in the food before threading it on.

{Metal Skewers}
Great for grilling and piling on chunks of meat and heavy vegetables. Opt for stainless-steel styles to prevent rusting.

{Wood Skewers}
Traditional wood skewers come in all shapes and sizes. Soak them in water before use so they don't catch fire on the grill.

{Cocktail Picks}
These mini sticks are perfect for olives and little nibbles. Made of metal, wood, or plastic, they're also ideal for meatballs and anything destined to be dunked into a cocktail.

{Bamboo Skewers}
These come in a variety of shapes and sizes. Choose heavier or thicker styles for larger pieces of food. Like rosemary and other wood skewers, soak these ahead of time.

{Popsicle Sticks}
Perfect for creamy frozen treats and all sorts of fruits, the flat shape holds food more securely and gives you and the little ones a better grip.

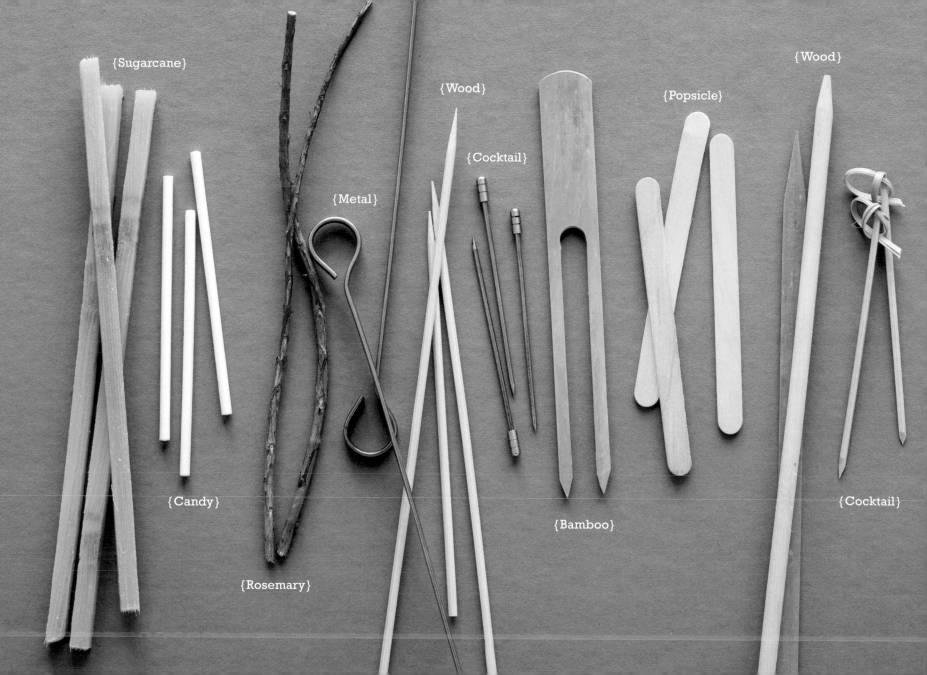

{Sugarcane}

{Wood}

{Wood}

{Popsicle}

{Cocktail}

{Metal}

{Candy}

{Bamboo}

{Cocktail}

{Rosemary}

Dips & Sauces

These versatile homemade condiments make good food on a stick even better. They can be store-bought or made at home in a matter of minutes. For my recipes, see Dips, Sauces, and Toppings (page 182).

{Peanut Sauce}
Nutty, sweet, and savory all at once, this sauce is right at home with grilled Asian food and vegetarian skewers.

{Tartar Sauce}
Creamy and savory, with a touch of sweetness, this classic is a wonderful accompaniment to fish and fried fare. I even love it with potato chips!

{Spicy Ketchup}
If everyday ketchup just doesn't do it for you, shake a few dashes of Tabasco into it to add some heat and tang. Your corn dogs will thank you!

{Honey-Mint Syrup}
Sweet, herbal, and perfect drizzled over fruit skewers. Consider this one a sophisticated sauce!

{Sauerkraut Relish}
I wouldn't dream of serving sausages on a stick without the sour tang of sauerkraut. It's great on sandwiches, too.

{Marinara Sauce}
A classic that belongs on pizza skewers and fried cheese. Don't forget about meatballs!

{Creamy Horseradish}
I like a sauce that gets my attention! The bite in this creamy topper works well with all sorts of fried and savory skewered foods.

{Sweet Chili Sauce}
I love the combination of heat-meets-sweet. Perfect with beef and pork and practically anything Asian inspired.

{Peanut Sauce}

{Tartar Sauce}

{Spicy Ketchup}

{Honey-Mint Syrup}

{Sauerkraut Relish}

{Marinara Sauce}

{Creamy Horseradish}

{Sweet Chili Sauce}

Dips & Sauces   11

{Mint Chutney}

{Spicy Buffalo Dipping Sauce}

{Mango Salsa}

{Green Goddess Dressing}

{Sweet and Fluffy Dipping Sauce}

{Garlic Butter}

{Honey Mustard}

{Cilantro Yogurt}

{Mint Chutney}

This British-sounding condiment is packed with fresh flavor. Pair it with lamb for a classic combination.

{Spicy Buffalo Dipping Sauce}

If you can find anything better than butter and hot sauce, please let me know. I love this stuff on practically anything!

{Mango Salsa}

Fresh chunks of mango and cilantro make a splendid condiment for fish and chicken skewers. I keep extra batches on hand—it's perfect with chips.

{Green Goddess Dressing}

I'm so happy this classic is back! Its flavors melds perfectly with those of young spring vegetables and delicate butter lettuce.

{Garlic Butter}

If there's one sauce that pairs with practically anything, it's this one. Rich butter, flecks of freshly chopped garlic . . . it's heavenly.

{Sweet and Fluffy Dipping Sauce}

Creamy and tangy, with a delightful sweetness. I must warn you: Make extra to drizzle and dip over all your fruit skewers.

{Honey Mustard}

This classic is a perfect foil to rich, salty–sweet skewers, like bacon-wrapped shrimp, and is excellent with vegetables, too. And the best part: It's a cinch to prepare.

{Cilantro Yogurt}

Quick, easy, and fresh. The perfect topper for skewered grilled vegetables, not to mention lamb and beef kebabs.

{Try dipping sweet treats in melted white or dark chocolate, whipped cream, or frosting.}

{Sherry Vinaigrette}

A high-quality sherry vinegar makes all the difference in this vinaigrette. And it's perfect for salads, too.

{Vanilla Frosting}

I'd spread this on just about anything if I could. Definitely bowl-licking worthy.

{Fresh Tomato Salsa}

The key to this salsa is rich, ripe, juicy tomatoes. I always keep it on hand.

{Spicy Garlic Soy}

This dipping sauce might have been created for Asian food, but it's stellar on so many things, meat and chicken included.

{Roasted Onion Dip}

The sweet, mellow, rich taste of roasted onions makes this one of my favorite dips ever.

{Chimichurri}

A classic Argentine sauce that makes a great marinade, too.

{Cucumber Yogurt}

Extremely easy sauce that's perfect with foods packed with heat and spice.

{Tamarind}

Sweet and slightly sour, this sauce is at home with Latin- and Asian-inspired skewers.

{Sherry Vinaigrette}

{Vanilla Frosting}

{Fresh Tomato Salsa}

{Spicy Garlic Soy}

{Roasted Onion Dip}

{Chimichurri}

{Cucumber Yogurt}

{Tamarind}

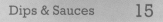

Dips & Sauces   15

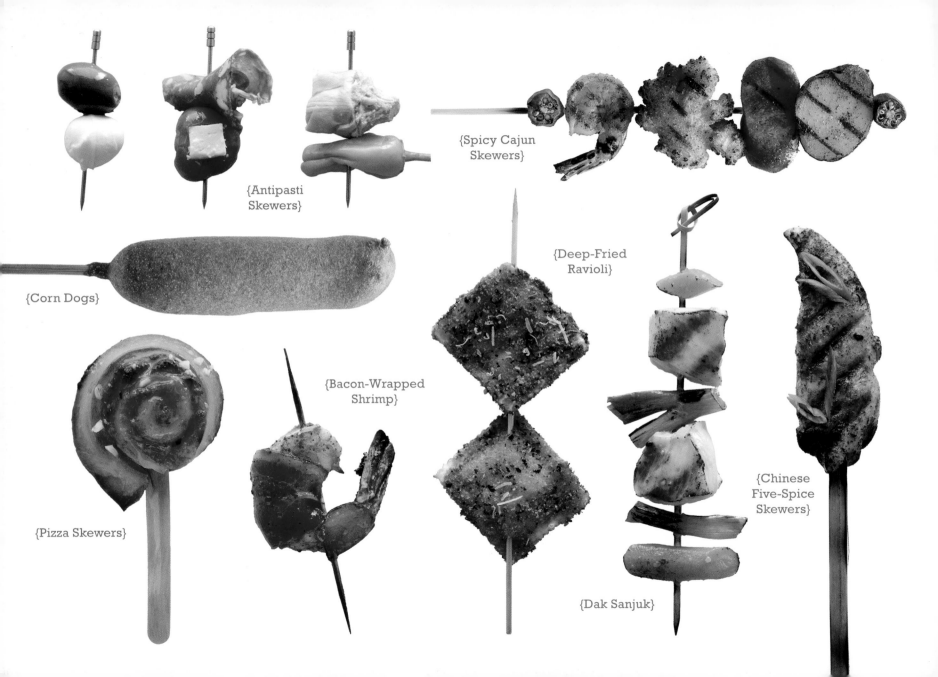

{Antipasti Skewers}

{Spicy Cajun Skewers}

{Corn Dogs}

{Deep-Fried Ravioli}

{Bacon-Wrapped Shrimp}

{Pizza Skewers}

{Dak Sanjuk}

{Chinese Five-Spice Skewers}

Savory Foods on a Stick

Antipasti Skewers

12 cocktail picks

½ cup pickled cherry peppers, stems and seeds removed

½ cup cubed feta (about ¼-inch cubes)

½ cup pepperoncini

½ cup pitted olives of your choice

½ cup marinated artichoke hearts

8 slices salami

I love last-minute get-togethers with friends. After shoving everything I own under my bed or in a closet, I often serve these antipasti skewers. They require no cooking, they're hard to mess up, and they take literally seconds to prepare. Plus, they make an elegant appetizer that's colorful and eye-catching—perfect for distracting guests from noticing that I didn't clean my house. *Serves 4*

1. Stuff cherry peppers with feta cubes.

2. Randomly stack peppers, pepperoncini, olives, artichoke hearts, and salami onto cocktail picks, varying combinations, until all picks are used. Serve.

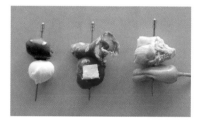

{Stuff, stack, and serve!}

Bacon-Wrapped Shrimp

with Honey Mustard Dipping Sauce

12 wooden cocktail picks

12 tiger shrimp, peeled and
    cleaned, with tails intact

Zest and juice of 1 lime

1 tsp chili powder

Pinch each salt and pepper

1 tbsp extra-virgin olive oil

6 strips thinly sliced applewood-
    smoked bacon, halved
    crosswise

Honey Mustard Dipping Sauce

½ cup mayonnaise

3 tbsp spicy brown mustard

2 tbsp honey

Pinch of cayenne pepper

Salt and white pepper, to taste

Quick: Name one ingredient that's better than bacon. See? You can't. And part of its beauty is that so many things—including these shrimp—are made infinitely more delicious when wrapped in this salty, smoky stuff. These morsels move fast at parties, so prepare an extra batch. It pays to use the highest quality bacon you can buy. *Serves 4*

1. Preheat oven to 375°F. Soak cocktail picks in water 30 minutes. Line a baking sheet with aluminum foil and coat lightly with nonstick oil spray; set aside.

2. Place shrimp, lime zest and juice, chili powder, salt, pepper, and oil in a bowl and toss gently. Cover and refrigerate at least 15 minutes and up to 1 hour. Remove cocktail picks from water.

3. Wrap each shrimp with half a slice of bacon and secure with a cocktail pick. Place skewers on prepared baking sheet and bake 20 minutes, turning skewers after 10 minutes. Broil 5 minutes. Serve hot.

4. **Make the sauce:** Whisk all ingredients in a small mixing bowl until blended. Cover and chill at least 1 hour. Before serving, let sauce rest at room temperature 20 minutes to allow flavors to meld.

{Bacon + Shrimp = Party!}

Beef and Vegetable Kebabs

12 bamboo skewers

2 tbsp vegetable oil

Marinade

⅓ cup extra-virgin olive oil

2 tbsp garlic powder

1 tbsp chili powder

1 tsp cumin

1 lb sirloin, cut into 1-inch cubes

1 cup cherry tomatoes

1 yellow onion, cut into
    1-inch pieces

1 green bell pepper, cut into
    1-inch pieces

Salt and pepper

Kebabs are Middle Eastern in origin, but they are enjoyed the world over. Preparation and ingredients vary, but they're always skewered and grilled. I love beef kebabs in warmer months, when the grill gets plenty of action. Pair them with a crisp green salad for a perfect summer repast. *Serves 4*

1. Soak skewers in water about 30 minutes. Heat grill or grill pan to medium-high and brush with vegetable oil.

2. Make the marinade: Whisk olive oil, garlic powder, chili powder, and cumin in a small bowl until well combined.

3. Place meat, tomatoes, onions, and peppers in a large bowl and add marinade, tossing to coat. Spear alternating pieces of meat and vegetables on skewers and season with salt and pepper to taste.

4. Grill skewers 6 to 8 minutes on each side. Serve warm.

Beef Skewers

with Chimichurri

12 bamboo skewers

2 tbsp extra-virgin
  olive oil

Chimichurri

½ cup extra-virgin olive oil

⅓ cup flat-leaf parsley, chopped

¼ cup red wine vinegar

2 tbsp basil leaves, chopped

2 tbsp oregano, chopped

2 tbsp minced shallots

2 garlic cloves, minced

1 tbsp crushed red
  pepper flakes

Salt and pepper to taste

1 lb skirt steak, thinly
  sliced against the grain

Salt and pepper

I'm a fan of skirt steak because it's usually cheaper than other cuts of meat. I'm also a big fan of Argentine chimichurri for its herbal, vinegary goodness. You can slice the meat and thread the skewers ahead of time, refrigerating them covered in plastic wrap until it's time to cook. Remember not to overcook the steak! *Serves 4*

1. Soak skewers in water about 30 minutes. Preheat grill or grill pan to medium-high and brush with oil.

2. Make the chimichurri: Place all chimichurri ingredients in a bowl and whisk until well combined. Set aside.

3. Thread steak pieces onto skewers and season with salt and pepper to taste. Grill skewers 3 to 5 minutes on each side.

4. Drizzle with chimichurri and serve with extra sauce on the side.

Beef Teriyaki

I've always preferred making beef teriyaki at home. I'm able to use the best meat, control the spiciness and sweetness, and, in this case, serve it on a stick. This is summer party food at its best. *Serves 4*

12 wood or metal skewers

2 tbsp vegetable oil

Teriykai Glaze

1 cup low-sodium soy sauce

½ cup brown sugar

2 tbsp honey

1 tbsp mirin

1 tsp minced ginger

1 tbsp minced garlic

1 tbsp cornstarch

½ lb sirloin, thinly sliced into 5-inch strips

2 tsp sesame oil

Salt and pepper

1. Soak skewers in water 30 minutes. Preheat grill or grill pan to medium-high and brush with vegetable oil.

2. Make the teriyaki glaze: In a small saucepan, stir together soy sauce, brown sugar, honey, mirin, ginger, and garlic. Simmer over medium heat 15 minutes. Meanwhile, stir cornstarch and ¼ cup cold water in a small bowl until cornstarch dissolves. Whisk cornstarch mixture into soy sauce mixture and continue simmering an additional 5 to 7 minutes, until thickened. Remove from heat and let cool.

3. In a bowl, toss beef strips with sesame oil. Thread each strip onto a skewer and season with salt and pepper to taste.

4. Grill skewers 5 minutes on each side. Then brush each with teriyaki glaze and grill an additional 4 minutes. Serve warm, brushed with additional glaze as desired.

Bò Lá Lôt

- 4 bamboo skewers
- 2 tbsp vegetable oil
- 2 garlic cloves, minced
- 1 shallot, minced
- 2 tbsp minced lemongrass
- 1 tbsp peeled and minced ginger
- 1 jalapeño, seeded and minced
- 1 lb lean ground beef
- Salt and pepper
- 2 tbsp Chinese five-spice powder
- 2 tbsp palm sugar (or dark brown sugar)
- 1 tsp fish sauce
- 2 tbsp vegetable oil
- 12 betel leaves

············{Tip}············
Flavorful Chinese five spice powder is known for its unique blend of star anise, pepper, cinnamon, clove, and ground fennel.

This Vietnamese dish is one of my all-time favorites: Seasoned ground meat is rolled inside betel leaves and grilled to smoky perfection. Betel leaves are sold at Asian markets; in a pinch, you can substitute grape or spinach leaves. But take my word: You'll definitely need an icy cold beer with these. *Serves 4*

1. Soak skewers in water about 30 minutes.

2. Place vegetable oil in a medium saucepan over medium-high heat. Add garlic, shallots, lemongrass, and ginger and cook, stirring occasionally, about 3 minutes. Add jalapeño and ground beef, breaking up meat with a wooden spoon. Season with salt and pepper to taste. Add Chinese five-spice powder, palm sugar, and fish sauce and cook, stirring occasionally, 5 to 7 minutes, or until meat is cooked through; remove from heat.

3. Preheat grill or grill pan to medium-high and brush with vegetable oil.

4. Lay betel leaves shiny side down and place 2 tablespoons of the meat mixture in the center of each. Fold in the sides, covering meat, and roll closed. Run skewers widthwise through stuffed leaves, 3 leaves per skewer. Brush each with olive oil and season with salt and pepper to taste.

5. Grill about 5 minutes on each side, or until leaves just begin to char. Serve warm.

Bratwursts

with Sauerkraut Relish and Creamy Horseradish Dipping Sauce

4 wooden skewers

Sauerkraut Relish

1 (14.5-ounce) can sauerkraut, drained and chopped

½ cup sugar

⅓ cup white wine vinegar

2 tbsp diced roasted red bell peppers

2 tbsp diced shallots

1 celery rib, diced

1 small carrot, peeled and diced

Creamy Horseradish Dipping Sauce

½ cup sour cream

¼ cup mayonnaise

¼ cup grated horseradish, or more to taste

1½ tbsp whole grain mustard

Zest and juice of ½ lemon

Salt and pepper

2 tbsp vegetable oil

4 bratwursts

There are no batters, no crunchy shells, no fancy dips here. Nothing but the tried-and-true taste of hearty bratwurst. So, it's best to use the highest quality brats you can find. If you're feeling adventurous, add a bit more grated horseradish to the dipping sauce—but be careful: The goal is to enjoy it, not to melt your face off. You'll also want tons of great German beer with these, but you're on your own with the oompah-pah. *Serves 4*

1. Soak skewers in water 30 minutes.

2. Make the sauerkraut relish: Place sauerkraut in a bowl. Combine sugar and vinegar in a saucepan and simmer over medium heat, stirring, until sugar dissolves. Pour mixture over sauerkraut, stir, and let cool. Fold in bell peppers, shallots, celery, and carrots. Cover and refrigerate at least 1 hour.

3. Make the dipping sauce: Whisk all horseradish sauce ingredients in a small bowl. Cover and refrigerate 30 minutes to 1 hour.

4. Heat grill or grill pan to medium-high and brush with vegetable oil. Slide bratwursts onto skewers and grill 6 minutes on each side. While brats are cooking, remove relish and horseradish sauce from refrigerator and allow to come to room temperature.

5. Reduce heat to medium and grill an additional 6 to 8 minutes. Serve warm, accompanied by relish and dipping sauce.

Breakfast Pancake Dogs

with Maple Syrup

8 wooden cocktail picks

5 cups vegetable oil

8 uncooked breakfast
    sausage links

Pancake Batter

1¼ cups all-purpose flour

1 tbsp sugar

1 tbsp light brown sugar

1 tsp baking powder

½ tsp baking soda

¼ tsp salt

⅛ tsp ground cinnamon

¾ cup buttermilk

¼ cup whole milk

1 egg

¼ cup maple syrup, for drizzling

The taste of sweet, syrupy pancakes meets savory, salty breakfast sausages in this hearty batter-coated link on a stick. I don't know about you, but I'm probably not going to wake up early enough to eat them for breakfast. Breakfast Pancake Dogs for dinner, anyone? *Serves 4*

1. Preheat oil in a large, heavy pot over medium-high heat. Thread each sausage link onto a pick. Set aside.

2. Make the pancake batter: Sift flour, sugars, baking powder, baking soda, salt, and cinnamon into a medium bowl.

3. Whisk buttermilk, whole milk, and egg in a separate bowl until well combined. Pour wet ingredients into dry ingredients and whisk gently until no lumps remain.

4. Once oil reaches 375°F, dip each sausage pick into batter, rolling to coat evenly, and carefully place entire pick in pot of oil. Fry in small batches about 5 minutes, or until golden.

5. Using tongs, remove sausage pick from oil and drain on paper towels. Serve hot, with a drizzle of maple syrup.

Caprese Sticks

12 cocktail picks

1 cup small fresh mozzarella balls (*ciliegine*)

½ cup cherry tomatoes

¼ cup sun-dried tomatoes

½ bunch fresh basil leaves

Sea salt and extra-virgin olive oil (optional)

These are based on a dish my dear friend Bobby once served at a party. While everyone else socialized, I secretly hung out in the kitchen next to the platter of these petite skewers, mesmerized by the combination of cheese and both fresh and sun-dried tomatoes. I ended up eating them all and then lying about it later. (Sorry, Bobby.) *Serves 4*

1. Arrange mozzarella balls, both kinds of tomatoes, and basil leaves onto cocktail picks, mixing and matching in varied combinations.

2. Before serving, sprinkle with sea salt and a quick drizzle of olive oil, if desired.

·············{Tip}·············
Caprese salad is a classic Italian first course that's irresistible on a stick!

Cheese Fondue

4 fondue forks

Cheese Sauce
1²/₃ cups dry white wine
1 garlic clove, minced
1 cup grated Gruyère cheese
1 cup grated Jarlsberg (or other Swiss) cheese
⅛ tsp pepper

1 cup French bread, cut into ½-inch cubes
1 cup cherry tomatoes
½ cup broccoli florets, blanched
½ cup cauliflower florets, blanched
½ cup quartered slices of salami

Cheese fondue may conjure up visions of shag carpeting and Burt Bacharach on the record player, but it's still one of my favorite party-pleasing menu items. Then again, anything involving hot, melted cheese shoots directly to the top of my list. I include suggested foods to pair with the fondue, but don't be afraid to come up with your own. *Serves 4*

1. Make the cheese sauce: Bring wine and garlic to a simmer in a medium saucepan; whisk in cheeses until sauce is smooth. Season with white pepper to taste.

2. Transfer to a fondue pot set over a lit candle. (If using an electric style, set it to low.)

3. Arrange bread, tomatoes, broccoli, cauliflower, and salami on a platter. Serve with forks alongside fondue pot, stirring sauce occasionally to maintain a smooth, uniform texture.

12 wooden skewers

12 chicken tenders

1½ cups buttermilk

2 tbsp tarragon, minced

1 tbsp thyme, minced

1 tsp cayenne pepper

1 cup all-purpose flour

1 tsp garlic powder

½ tsp onion powder

2 tsp salt

1 tsp black pepper

3 cups vegetable oil

Salt and pepper

Waffle Batter

2¼ cups all-purpose flour

1 cup plus 2 tbsp milk

¼ cup plus 2 tbsp vegetable oil

3 tsp sugar

3 tsp vanilla extract

1¼ tsp baking powder

½ tsp baking soda

½ tsp salt

1½ eggs, beaten

¼ cup (½ stick) butter, melted

⅓ cup maple syrup

Chicken and Waffles

I've developed a deep appreciation for gloriously fried chicken served atop a golden waffle, an American favorite available at a chain of restaurants known as Roscoe's Chicken and Waffles. Though it might take a bit of time to wrap your mind around this concept, trust me: It's delicious. This version re-creates those great flavors and puts it all, yes, on a stick. *Serves 4*

1. Fold together chicken tenders, buttermilk, tarragon, thyme, and cayenne pepper in a shallow dish until thoroughly combined. Cover and refrigerate overnight.

2. Remove chicken mixture from refrigerator. Sift flour, garlic powder, onion powder, salt, and pepper into a separate shallow dish.

3. Preheat oil in a large cast-iron pan over medium-high heat. Thread each tender onto a skewer.

4. Once oil reaches 350°F, dredge each skewered tender in flour mixture, coating completely and shaking off excess. Dip each back in buttermilk mixture and again in flour mixture, gently shaking off excess.

5. In small batches, gently drop skewers into oil and fry about 5 minutes. Flip and fry an additional 3 to 5 minutes, until golden brown. Drain on paper towels and season with salt and pepper to taste.

6. Make the waffle batter: Place all waffle batter ingredients in a large bowl and whisk until no lumps remain. Dip fried tenders in batter, coating completely. In batches, gently drop skewers back into oil and fry about 4 minutes. Flip and fry an additional 3 to 4 minutes. Drain on paper towels.

7. Just before serving, brush with a light coating of melted butter and drizzle with maple syrup. Serve warm.

8 bamboo skewers

Marinade
½ cup sugar
⅓ cup dry-roasted peanuts
¼ cup soy sauce
2 tbsp ground turmeric
4 garlic cloves, roughly chopped
½ stalk lemongrass, roughly chopped
2 tbsp peeled and roughly chopped galangal

1 lb boneless skinless chicken thighs, cut into 1-inch cubes
2 tbsp vegetable oil

Peanut Dipping Sauce
¼ cup vegetable oil
½ cup dry-roasted peanuts
2 kaffir lime leaves, roughly chopped
2 cloves garlic, roughly chopped
1 serrano chili, roughly chopped
2 tablespoons soy sauce
¼ cup reserved marinade
Salt
1 scallion, thinly sliced

Chicken Satay

with Peanut Dipping Sauce

Travel around the world and you'll find many variations of this dish, all of them equally delicious. My version uses chicken thighs, which I find so much juicier and more flavorful than chicken breasts. Galangal, a relative of ginger, gives the marinade an intriguing floral taste. Serve these with mounds of fluffy white rice—it makes a sensational supper. *Serves 4*

1. Stir all marinade ingredients with ⅓ cup water until well blended; reserve ¼ cup for use in peanut dipping sauce. Pour remaining marinade over chicken; cover and refrigerate 6 to 24 hours.

2. Soak skewers in water 30 minutes.

3. Remove marinated chicken from refrigerator. Preheat grill or grill pan to medium-high and grease with oil.

4. Thread chicken onto skewers. Grill 5 to 6 minutes, then flip and cook another 5 to 6 minutes, until cooked through. Serve hot with peanut dipping sauce.

5. Make the sauce: Preheat oil in a saucepan over medium-high heat. Add peanuts, lime leaves, garlic, and serrano chili and cook, stirring occasionally, until fragrant, about 5 minutes. Stir in coconut milk and soy sauce and continue cooking another 5 minutes.

6. Lower heat to medium and stir in 1/4 cup water and the reserved marinade. Season with salt to taste. Remove from heat and let cool briefly before pouring into a blender or food processor; puree until smooth.

7. Return sauce to saucepan and simmer over low heat, stirring occasionally, about 5 minutes. Pour into a bowl and top with scallions.

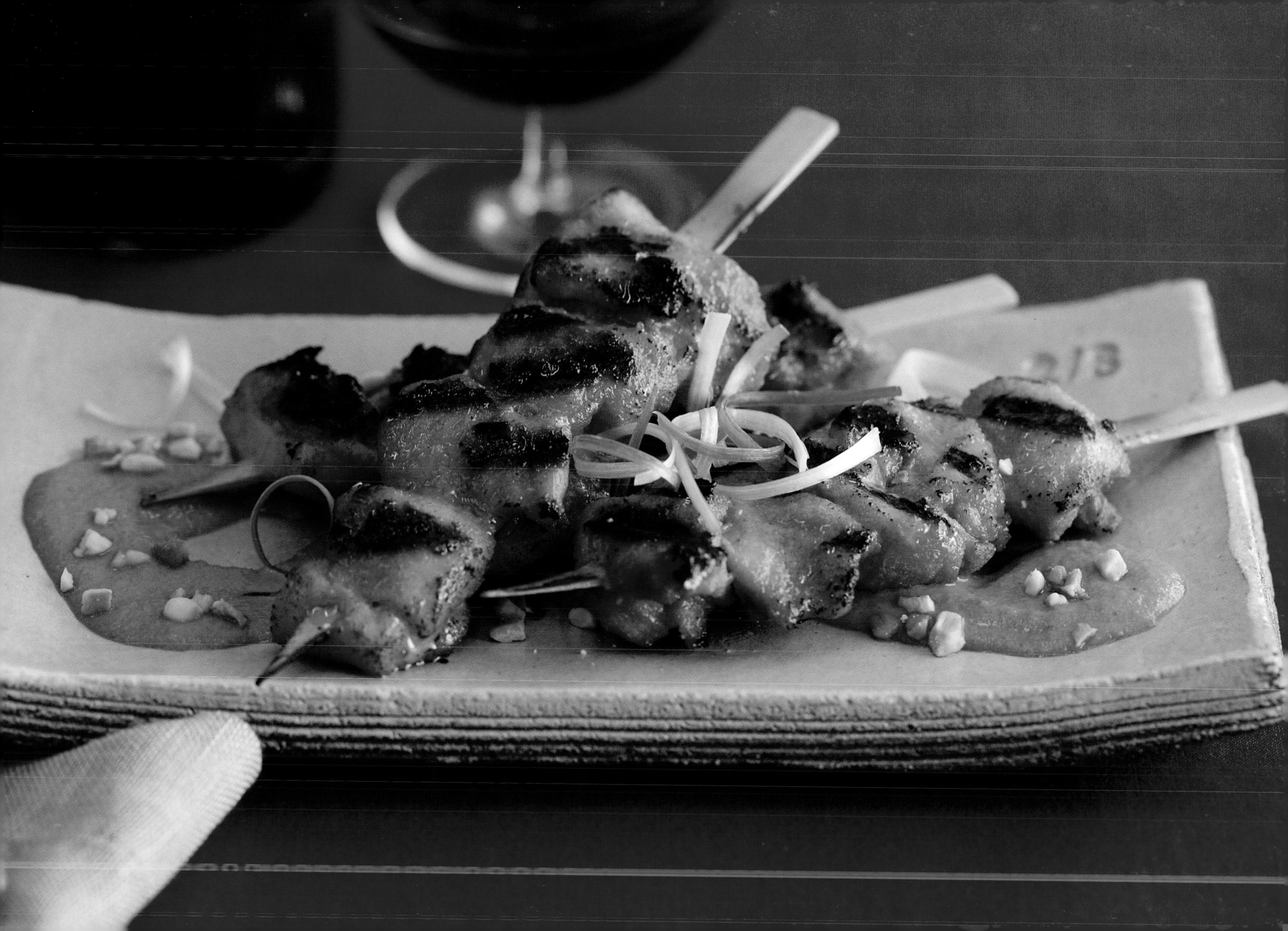

Chinese Five-Spice Skewers

12 wooden skewers

Marinade
2 tbsp Chinese five-spice powder
1 tbsp light brown sugar
1 tbsp minced lemongrass
1 tbsp sesame oil
2 tsp ground cumin
2 tsp crushed red pepper flakes
1 tsp salt
½ tsp pepper
⅓ cup extra-virgin olive oil

12 chicken tenders
2 tbsp olive oil
Salt and pepper

I'm completely addicted to the flavors of Chinese five-spice powder, an intriguing blend that includes cloves, star anise, cinnamon, pepper, and ground fennel. It's perfect for these chicken skewers, which make a simple but satisfying meal when paired with white rice and an Asian cucumber salad. *Serves 4*

1. Whisk all marinade ingredients in a small bowl. Place chicken tenders in a shallow dish and fold in marinade until fully combined. Cover and refrigerate about 1 hour, turning tenders halfway through.

2. Meanwhile, soak skewers in water at least 30 minutes. Heat grill or grill pan to medium-high and brush with oil.

3. Remove tenders from refrigerator and thread onto skewers. Grill about 7 minutes, flip, and cook an additional 5 to 6 minutes. (Depending on the size of your grill, you may want to work in two batches; if so, brush grill surface with half the oil before cooking each batch.) Season with salt and pepper to taste and serve hot.

············{Tip}············
This marinade works wonders on chicken, even when it's not served on a stick.

12 wooden cocktail picks

1 qt vegetable oil

Meatballs

¾ lb lean ground pork or turkey

2 tbsp low-sodium soy sauce

1 tbsp oyster sauce

1 tbsp minced garlic

2 tsp peeled and minced ginger

1 tsp ground cumin

½ tsp ground cinnamon

½ bunch cilantro, minced

1 scallion, thinly sliced

Salt and pepper, to taste

Sweet-and-Sour Chili Sauce

1 cup rice wine vinegar

1 cup sugar

2 tbsp minced lemongrass

½ bunch mint, minced

2 tbsp cilantro, minced

1 tbsp minced garlic

1 tbsp seeded and minced red
    jalapeño

1 tsp peeled and minced ginger

Chinese Meatballs
with Sweet-and-Sour Chili Sauce

I should call these the Great Disappearing Chinese Meatballs, because they vanish every time I set them out. Maybe it's the dipping sauce that makes them so fun, or maybe it's the sticks. Whatever it is, these bite-size treats were made for parties. And my mouth. *Serves 4*

1. Preheat oil in a large, heavy pot over medium-high heat.

2. Mix all meatball ingredients in a large bowl, using your hands to thoroughly combine, until mixture begins to get sticky. Form into 12 small, even balls.

3. Once oil reaches 350°F, drop in half the meatballs and fry about 5 minutes; drain on a paper towel. Repeat with remaining meatballs. Thread a cocktail pick through each one.

4. Make the sweet-and-sour chili sauce: Stir vinegar, sugar, and lemongrass in a saucepan over medium heat and cook until sugar dissolves and liquid reduces by one-third. Strain into a bowl and cool completely. Stir in mint, cilantro, garlic, red jalapeño, and ginger. Serve warm or at room temperature, alongside meatballs.

4 bamboo skewers

Mango Salsa
2 mangoes, peeled and diced
2 tbsp cilantro, minced
2 tbsp diced red onion
1 tbsp seeded and diced jalapeño
1 tsp minced garlic
Zest and juice of 1 lime
1 tsp extra-virgin olive oil
Salt

12 tiger shrimp, cleaned and
    peeled with tails intact
Salt and pepper
3/4 cup all-purpose flour
2 tsp garlic powder
1 tsp cayenne pepper
1 egg
3/4 cup unsweetened coconut
    flakes
1/4 cup almond meal
2 tbsp panko bread crumbs
1 qt vegetable oil

Coconut Shrimp
with Mango Salsa

Coconut-flavored shrimp with mango salsa is a lucky little recipe: It's fruity and fun, but feels like elegant and luxurious at the same time. During the summer months, I always have fresh mango salsa on hand—it's wonderful with pork, chicken, and all types of seafood. You can even enjoy it on a chip. Its versatility can't be beat. *Serves 4*

1. Line a baking sheet with parchment paper.

2. Toss salsa ingredients in a bowl, seasoning with salt to taste. Cover and refrigerate until ready to serve.

3. Season shrimp with salt and pepper. Combine flour, garlic powder, and cayenne pepper in a shallow dish; beat egg in a separate dish; in a third dish, combine coconut, almond meal, and panko.

4. Dredge shrimp first in flour mixture, shaking off excess, and then dip in egg. Dredge in coconut mixture, gently shaking off excess.

5. Thread 3 shrimp per skewer. Place skewers on the prepared baking sheet and refrigerate 1 hour.

6. After shrimp have chilled, preheat oil in a large, heavy pot over medium-high heat. Once oil reaches 350°F, gently drop skewers into pot and fry about 6 to 8 minutes, or until golden. Drain on a paper towel and season with salt and pepper to taste. Serve warm, with mango salsa on the side.

Corn Dogs

4 wooden skewers

1 qt vegetable oil

3/4 cup all-purpose flour

3/4 cup cornmeal

2 tbsp sugar

1/2 tsp baking powder

1/8 tsp baking soda

1 tsp salt

1/8 tsp black pepper

3/4 cup whole milk

1 egg

4 jumbo hot dogs

Ketchup and yellow mustard,
    for serving

Be still my heart! I could easily devote every page of this cookbook to the corn dog, but something tells me you'd tire of it. At any rate, I don't believe there's such a thing as a bad corn dog. It is the quintessential food on a stick, and because it's highly adaptable—substituting sausages or veggie dogs for standard wieners—the options are endless. *Serves 4*

1. Preheat oil in a large, heavy pot over medium-high heat.

2. Mix flour, cornmeal, sugar, baking powder, baking soda, salt, and pepper in a bowl. Stir in milk and egg and whisk gently until fully combined.

3. Once oil reaches 360°F, thread hot dogs onto skewers. Dip each in batter, rolling until fully coated, and quickly drop entire stick into oil. Fry, 2 at a time, 4 to 5 minutes. Drain on paper towels. Repeat for remaining corn dogs. Serve warm, accompanied by ketchup and mustard.

·········{Tip}··········

For veggie dogs, replace egg with 1/4 cup Egg Beaters and whole milk with almond milk.

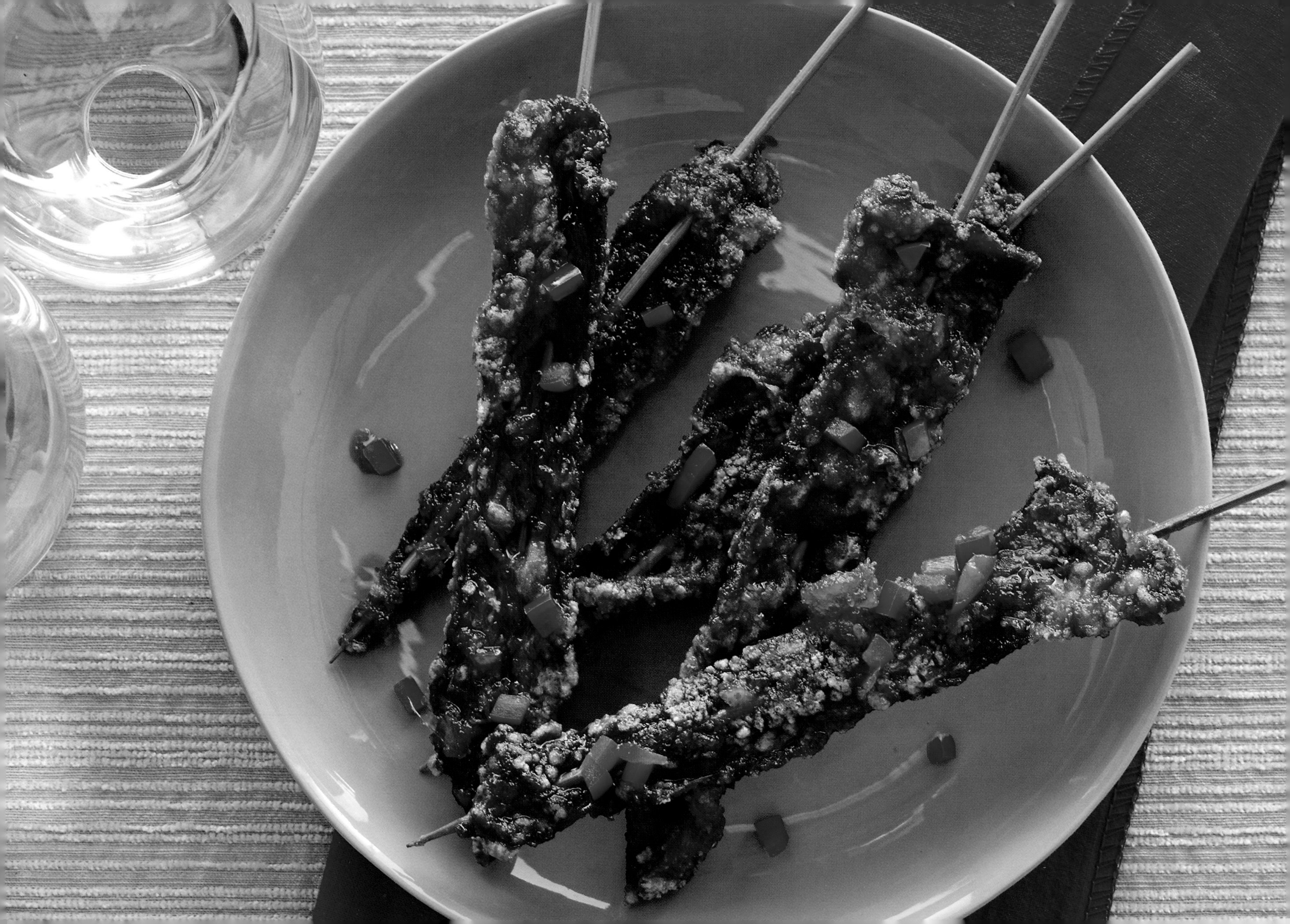

Crispy Orange Beef Skewers

Magic happens to flank steak when it's lightly dusted in cornstarch and then fried. Coating the crispy, savory ribbons of meat in a sweet orange glaze makes them irresistible. Serve with a side of rice for a light lunch or dinner. *Serves 4*

16 bamboo skewers

5 qt vegetable oil

1¼ lb flank steak, thinly sliced against the grain

¼ cup cornstarch

Orange Glaze

¼ cup rice wine vinegar

3 tbsp low-sodium soy sauce

2 tbsp sugar

2 tbsp orange marmalade

1 tbsp freshly squeezed orange juice

1 tbsp honey

2 tbsp extra-virgin olive oil

1 tbsp minced ginger

1 tbsp orange zest

1 garlic clove, minced

············{Tip}············
Top with more orange glaze and fresh chopped bell peppers, if desired.

1. Preheat oil in a large, heavy pot over medium-high heat.

2. Toss steak with cornstarch and shake off excess; let rest 15 minutes.

3. Make the orange glaze: Whisk vinegar, soy sauce, sugar, marmalade, juice, and honey in a small bowl. Heat oil in a skillet over medium-high heat. Add ginger, orange zest, and garlic and cook, stirring occasionally, about 2 minutes, or until slightly thickened. Pour soy sauce mixture into skillet and cook, stirring, 3 to 5 minutes, or until slightly thickened.

4. Thread beef onto skewers. Once oil reaches 350°F, carefully place skewers in pot and fry 3 to 5 minutes, or until browned and crispy. Drain on paper towels. Pour orange glaze over meat and toss gently until well coated. Serve hot.

12 small bamboo skewers

Latin Green Goddess Dressing
¾ cup mayonnaise
¾ cup Mexican crema
    (or sour cream)
½ cup roughly chopped cilantro
1 tbsp tarragon vinegar
Zest of half a lime
1 tbsp fresh lime juice
2 scallions, thinly sliced
1 pickled jalapeño, seeded
    and roughly chopped
Salt and pepper

1 cup baby summer squash
    (yellow and green), tops
    and bottoms trimmed
1 cup small radishes, peeled on
    two sides
½ cup baby portabella mush-
    rooms, cleaned and cut
    into quarters
½ cup sliced sweet red and
    yellow peppers (½-inch
    pieces)
2 endives, sliced into ½-inch
    pieces
2 celery stalks, sliced into
    1-inch pieces

Crudité Skewers
with Latin Green Goddess Dressing

I went through a green goddess phase about a year ago, using it regularly as a dressing for salads or as a dip for anything edible I could get my hands on. I won't say I burned out on it, but I was inspired to create my own version of this classic California dip, infused with just a touch of Latin flavor. If you can't find Mexican crema at your local Latin market, you can happily substitute sour cream. *Serves 4*

1. Make the Latin green goddess dressing: Place all dressing ingredients in a food processor and process about 1 minute, or until smooth. Cover and refrigerate at least 30 minutes, or until ready to serve.

2. Skewer vegetables in random combinations. Serve with chilled dressing.

Dak Sanjuk

8 wooden skewers
2 tbsp vegetable oil

Marinade
2 garlic cloves, minced
1½ tbsp sherry
1 tbsp toasted sesame seeds
1 tbsp sesame oil
1 tbsp extra-virgin olive oil

2 small boneless skinless chicken
    breasts, cut into 1-inch cubes
16 baby carrots, blanched
4 scallions, sliced into 1-inch
    pieces
Salt and pepper

This traditional Korean recipe couldn't be easier or more flavorful: Tender chunks of chicken are marinated and skewered with carrots and scallions. The addition of sherry gives this dish a sweet, elegant note. *Serves 4*

1. Soak skewers in water 30 minutes. Preheat grill or grill pan to medium-high and brush with vegetable oil.

2. Whisk all marinade ingredients in a small bowl. Set aside.

3. Toss chicken, carrots, and scallions in a bowl. Fold in marinade until all pieces are well coated.

4. Thread chicken and vegetables onto skewers, alternating ingredients. Season with salt and pepper to taste. Grill 7 to 8 minutes on each side. Serve warm.

Deep-Fried Mac 'n' Cheese

4 bamboo skewers

Mac 'n' Cheese Squares
2 tbsp unsalted butter
2 tbsp all-purpose flour
1 cup milk
2/3 cup grated sharp cheddar
   cheese
1/3 cup grated white cheddar
   cheese
1/4 cup grated fontina cheese
1/2 lb dried elbow macaroni,
   cooked and drained
Salt and pepper

5 qt vegetable oil
1 cup all-purpose flour
2 eggs, lightly beaten
2 cups panko bread crumbs
Salt and pepper

············{Tip}············
This recipe makes 9 mac 'n'
cheese squares, enough for 4
skewers—plus one for the chef.

I'll admit there's a certain amount of culinary bravado required to pull off these crunchy squares of scrumptious mac 'n' cheese. It's not for the faint of heart. So who *is* it for? Those who enjoy excess and deep-fried indulgence. Count me in! *Serves 4*

1. Grease an 8-by-8-inch baking dish with cooking spray.

2. Melt butter in a saucepan over medium heat and whisk in flour until smooth; continue whisking 4 minutes and then add milk in a slow, steady stream until fully combined. Cook 4 to 5 minutes, until mixture has thickened but is not brown; stir occasionally to prevent lumps and burning.

3. Once thickened, stir in cheeses a handful at a time until all is incorporated and mixture is smooth.

4. Fold cheese sauce into cooked macaroni to coat completely. Season with salt and pepper to taste. Pour into prepared dish, pressing pasta firmly with the back of a spoon. Cover with plastic wrap and refrigerate at least 3 hours or up to 1 day. Once pasta has set, cut into 9 equal squares. Freeze about 1 hour.

5. Preheat oil in a large, heavy pot over medium-high heat.

6. Place flour, eggs, and panko in three separate shallow dishes. Dredge frozen pasta squares first in flour, shaking off excess, then in egg, and finally in panko, coating fully. Thread 2 squares onto each skewer.

7. Once oil reaches 350°F, carefully place skewers in pot and fry about 6 minutes, or until golden brown. Drain on paper towels and lightly season with salt and pepper to taste. Serve hot.

4 wooden skewers

Marinara Sauce
1 tbsp olive oil
1 garlic clove, minced
1 (14.5-ounce) can whole tomatoes, drained, seeded, and roughly chopped
¼ cup dry red wine
2 tbsp fresh oregano, minced
2 tbsp sugar
Salt and pepper

1 qt vegetable oil
1 cup all-purpose flour
2 eggs, beaten
1 cup plain bread crumbs
½ cup grated Parmesan cheese, divided
2 tbsp dried oregano
2 tbsp dried basil
1 tbsp dried thyme
2 tsp garlic powder
1 tsp salt
½ tsp pepper
12 store-bought ravioli

Deep-Fried Ravioli
with Marinara Sauce

This recipe is a great twist on traditional ravioli. Frying gives the ravioli a satisfying crunch that contrasts nicely with their soft interiors. You can make ravioli from scratch or go the quick store-bought route, choosing from among the high-quality refrigerated versions readily available. If you're a purist and don't think ravioli should be fried or stuck on a stick, try it. You just might change your mind. *Serves 4*

1. Make the marinara sauce: Warm oil in a medium pot over medium heat. Add garlic and tomatoes and cook 5 minutes, stirring occasionally. Deglaze pot by adding wine, stirring to loosen browned bits from bottom of pot; then stir in oregano and sugar and season with salt and pepper to taste. Transfer mixture to a food processor and process to desired consistency. Return mixture to pot and simmer 30 minutes. Cool slightly before serving.

2. Preheat vegetable oil in a large, heavy pot over medium-high heat.

3. Place flour in one shallow dish and eggs in another. In a third, mix bread crumbs, ¼ cup Parmesan, oregano, basil, thyme, garlic powder, salt, and pepper.

4. In two batches, toss ravioli in flour, gently shaking off excess. Dip in egg and then in bread crumb mixture. Thread 3 breaded ravioli onto each skewer.

5. Once oil reaches 350°F, carefully place skewers in pot, 2 at a time, and fry about 4 to 5 minutes. Drain on paper towels and sprinkle with remaining ¼ cup Parmesan. Serve warm, with marinara sauce on the side.

Elote

4 wooden sticks

4 ears fresh corn, shucked

¼ cup mayonnaise

½ cup grated Parmesan cheese

2 tsp chili powder

4 lime wedges

Salt (optional)

Throughout Mexican neighborhoods and urban centers you'll find one of my favorite street foods: skewered boiled or grilled corn that's slathered with mayonnaise, Parmesan cheese, and chili powder. It is heavenly. The combination might sound unlikely, but just wait until your tongue tastes it. You'll soon realize what you've been missing. *Serves 4*

1. Boil corn 4 minutes or to desired doneness; drain. Insert a wooden stick firmly into the bottom of each ear.

2. Spread 1 tablespoon mayonnaise on each ear and sprinkle with 2 tablespoons Parmesan and ½ teaspoon chili powder. Squeeze a wedge of lime over each and season with salt, if desired. Eat them on the go!

8 wooden skewers

1 gallon vegetable oil

⅓ cup cornstarch

Beer Batter

1 cup all-purpose flour

1 tsp baking powder

1 tsp salt

1 tsp ground sage

½ tsp ground black pepper

½ tsp cayenne pepper

¼ tsp chili powder

1 bottle Guinness or other dark beer (do not open until ready to use)

4 Kennebec potatoes, cut into ½-inch pieces

Salt and pepper

4 (1½-ounce) strips Alaskan cod

Lemon wedges for serving (optional)

·········{Tip}·········
Sure, you can substitute your choice of potatoes, but Kennebecs—with their thin skin and white flesh—were *made* for frying.

Fish and Chips

I'll be the first to tell you that Americans don't eat enough fish and chips. I'd like to remedy that problem by encouraging you to transform this on-a-plate dish to one that's on a stick. It requires a bit of work, but the results are totally worth it. Newspaper is optional. *Serve 4*

1. Preheat oil in a large pot over medium-high heat. Place cornstarch in a shallow dish; set aside.

2. Combine all batter ingredients except beer in a large bowl; set aside.

3. Slide 2 or 3 potato slices onto each of 4 skewers. Season lightly with salt and pepper. Once oil reaches 350°F, carefully place skewers in pot and fry 5 minutes. Drain on paper towels.

4. While potatoes are frying, thread 1 strip of fish onto each of the remaining 4 skewers. Roll in cornstarch and shake to remove excess; set aside.

5. Whisk beer into flour mixture until fully incorporated; batter should be thick and bubbly. Dip and roll fish skewers 2 at a time in batter; carefully place in pot of oil, and fry about 6 minutes, or until golden. Drain on paper towels and season with salt and pepper to taste.

6. Return potato skewers to oil and fry an additional 8 to 10 minutes. Drain on paper towels and season again with salt and pepper. Serve with the fish skewers and lemon wedges, if desired.

6 short wooden skewers

Tartar Sauce

3/4 cup mayonnaise

2 tbsp sour cream

2 tbsp minced cornichons

2 tbsp capers, minced

1/2 tsp sugar

Zest and juice of 1 lemon

Salt and pepper

1 qt vegetable oil

1 lb cod fillets, poached
    and flaked

2/3 cup plain bread crumbs

2 tbsp minced tarragon

1 tbsp minced flat-leaf parsley

1 tbsp garlic powder

2 tbsp thinly sliced chives

1 tsp cayenne pepper

1 egg

Salt and pepper

1 cup panko bread crumbs

1/4 cup grated Parmesan cheese

Lemon wedges, for serving

Fish Balls

with Tartar Sauce

If you're like me and you think fried things taste even better when dipped into creamy sauces, then this recipe is for you. It's a riff on classic fried fish and tartar sauce in which panko bread crumbs add the perfect crunch. Don't forget a squeeze of lemon just before serving. *Serves 4*

1. Make the tartar sauce: Stir all sauce ingredients in a small bowl until thoroughly combined. Cover and refrigerate about 1 hour. About 15 minutes before eating, remove sauce from refrigerator and let sit at room temperature; stir just before serving.

2. Preheat oil in a large, heavy pot over medium-high heat.

3. Place cod, bread crumbs, tarragon, parsley, garlic powder, chives, cayenne pepper, and egg in a bowl and mix until thoroughly combined. Season with salt and pepper to taste. Form fish mixture into 12 equal balls (about the size of a golf ball).

4. Combine panko and Parmesan in a shallow dish. Roll fish balls in panko mixture and coat well. Thread 2 balls onto each skewer.

5. Once oil reaches 350°F, carefully place skewers in pot and fry, in batches, 4 to 6 minutes. Drain on paper towels and season with salt and pepper. Serve warm, with tartar sauce and lemon wedges.

Fried Mozzarella

with Marinara Sauce

12 cocktail picks

1 qt vegetable oil

1 cup all-purpose flour

2 eggs

1½ cups Italian seasoned bread crumbs

½ cup panko bread crumbs

¼ cup grated Parmesan cheese

1 lb part-skim fresh mozzarella, sliced 1 inch thick and then into triangles

Salt and pepper

Marinara sauce (see page 59), for serving

·············{Tip}···········

Panko bread crumbs are made from crustless bread. They're particularly airy, crunchy, and good for frying!

Can you think of anything better than fried cheese? I certainly can't. If I had my druthers, I'd eat these golden cheesey triangles every day of the week. Dipped in marinara sauce, they make a fantastic starter or party food. Be sure to serve them immediately to take full advantage of their melty, oozy goodness. *Serves 4*

1. Preheat oil in a large, heavy pot over medium-high heat.

2. Place flour in a shallow dish. Beat eggs in a separate shallow dish. Place seasoned bread crumbs, panko, and Parmesan in a third shallow dish and mix until well combined.

3. Dredge mozzarella pieces first in flour, shaking off excess; then dip in egg and dredge in bread crumb mixture until fully coated.

4. Once oil reaches 350°F, gently drop mozzarella pieces, a few at a time, in pot and fry until golden, 6 to 8 minutes. Drain on paper towels and season lightly with salt and pepper. Pierce each with a cocktail pick and serve with marinara sauce.

12 cocktail picks

5 qt vegetable oil

1 cup all-purpose flour

2 eggs, lightly beaten

2 cups seasoned bread crumbs

1 cup baby portabella mushrooms, cleaned and stems trimmed

1 cup button mushrooms, cleaned and stems trimmed

Salt and pepper

Roasted Onion Dip

1/2 cup extra-virgin olive oil

1 yellow onion, diced

4 sweet onions, roasted

1/2 cup cream cheese, at room temperature

1/4 cup sour cream

3 tbsp mayonnaise

1 garlic clove, roughly chopped

Salt and pepper

············{Tip}············

To roast onions, quarter them and toss in 3 tbsp extra-virgin olive oil, salt, and pepper. Roast at 350°F in a baking dish for about 45 minutes or until translucent and falling apart.

Fried Mushrooms

with Roasted Onion Dip

Battered and fried mushrooms are earthy and full of *umami*—and they're right at home on a stick. Dip them into savory roasted onion dip for added flavor. *Serves 4*

1. Preheat oil in a large, heavy pot over medium-high heat. Line a baking sheet with parchment paper.

2. Place flour, eggs, and bread crumbs in separate shallow dishes. Toss mushrooms in flour and shake off excess. Dip in egg and then dredge in bread crumbs until fully coated. Arrange in a single layer on the prepared baking sheet and freeze about 15 minutes.

3. When oil reaches 350°F, gently drop mushrooms in pot and fry 6 to 8 minutes, or until golden. Drain on a paper towel, skewer, and season with salt and pepper to taste.

4. Make the dip: Warm oil in a medium skillet over medium heat. Add yellow onion and cook until golden brown and crispy, 8 to 10 minutes. Drain onions on a paper towel and reserve 1/4 cup of the cooking oil.

5. Place reserved cooking oil, roasted sweet onions, cream cheese, sour cream, mayonnaise, and garlic in a food processor and process until smooth. Season with salt and pepper to taste.

6. Transfer mixture to a bowl, fold in all but 2 tablespoons of the fried onions, and refrigerate 30 minutes. Once chilled, pour into a serving bowl and top with the reserved fried onions.

Fried Pickles

with Ranch Dressing

8 wooden cocktail picks

1 qt vegetable oil

$2/3$ cup all-purpose flour

1 tsp cayenne pepper

2 eggs

2 tbsp buttermilk

1 tbsp dill, minced

$1^1/2$ cups seasoned bread crumbs

8 gherkins

8 cocktail onions

8 pickle chips

Salt and pepper

1 cup store-bought ranch dressing

............{Tip}............

Homemade dips are lovely, but sometimes a good store-bought ranch hits the spot.

If you've never tried fried pickles, you're in for a treat. A staple of state fairs countrywide, these crunchy nuggets might seem like an oddity—until you take that first bite. The heat tempers the pickles' vinegary-ness, resulting in a mellow, almost zucchini-like taste. I've kicked it up a notch by pairing sweet gherkins with cocktail onions and pickle chips. This trio of fried snacks skewered on a stick makes for a beautiful presentation. *Serves 4*

1. Preheat oil in a large, heavy pot over medium-high heat.

2. Mix flour and cayenne pepper in a shallow dish. In a medium bowl, whisk eggs, buttermilk, and dill. Place bread crumbs in a second shallow dish.

3. Thread 1 gherkin, 1 cocktail onion, and 1 pickle chip on each cocktail pick. Once oil reaches 350°F, toss skewers in flour mixture, shaking off excess; dip in egg and then dredge in bread crumbs until fully coated.

4. Drop skewers gently into oil and fry 4 to 5 minutes. Drain on paper towels and season with salt and pepper to taste. Serve with ranch dressing.

Ground Shrimp on Sugarcane

12 sticks sugarcane

3 tbsp vegetable oil

Ground Shrimp Balls

1½ lb tiger shrimp, cleaned and peeled

1⅓ cups panko bread crumbs

½ bunch cilantro, roughly chopped

1 stalk lemongrass, roughly chopped

3 tbsp peeled and minced ginger

2 garlic cloves, minced

1 red jalapeño, minced

1 egg white, lightly beaten

3 tbsp low-sodium soy sauce

2 tbsp light brown sugar

2 tsp fish sauce

Salt and pepper

Flavorful ground shrimp seasoned with herbs and fish sauce is imbued with an added dimension when cooked on sugarcane. As you eat these skewers, make sure to do one thing: Chew the sugarcane, and enjoy its sweet flavor. *Serves 4*

1. Preheat grill or grill pan to medium-high and brush with oil.

2. Place shrimp ball ingredients in a food processor and pulse a few times until almost smooth, with some chunks remaining. Season with salt and pepper.

3. Scoop about 2½ tablespoons of shrimp mixture and form into an oval meatball around 1 sugarcane stick. Repeat for remaining shrimp mixture and sugarcane.

4. Grill skewers 3 to 4 minutes on each side. Serve hot.

Korean-Style BBQ Pork Belly Skewers

16 bamboo skewers

Pork Marinade
1/3 cup Korean chili paste
    (gochujang)
2 1/2 tbsp sugar
2 tbsp low-sodium soy sauce
2 tbsp Korean chili powder
    (gochugaru)
2 tbsp sesame oil
2 scallions, thinly sliced
2 garlic cloves, minced

1 (1-lb piece) pork belly, cut in
    half widthwise
2 tbsp vegetable oil
1 cup cooked white rice
8 leaves red-leaf lettuce
1 scallion, thinly sliced
2 tbsp toasted sesame seeds

I'd love to share the story of my first time making pork belly (the unsalted, fresh side of pork), at home all alone, but then I'd have to admit that I ate two whole pounds of it in a single sitting. This recipe might require a visit to your local Korean market, but who knows—maybe you'll make friends along the way, so you won't end up eating an insane amount of pork belly all by yourself. *Serves 4*

1. Soak skewers in water about 30 minutes.

2. Make the marinade: Place all marinade ingredients in a bowl and whisk until well combined. Add pork belly and toss gently to coat. Refrigerate at least 1 hour and up to 24 hours.

3. Preheat grill or grill pan to high and brush with oil. Thread pork belly onto skewers. Shake off excess marinade and grill 2 to 3 minutes on each side.

4. To serve, place 2 tablespoons of rice on each lettuce leaf. Top with 1 pork belly skewer and finish with a sprinkle of scallions and sesame seeds.

8 bamboo skewers

Mint Chutney
1 cup mint, roughly chopped
½ cup cilantro leaves, roughly chopped
¼ red onion, roughly chopped
4 tbsp Greek yogurt
2 tbsp lemon juice
Salt and pepper

2 tbsp vegetable oil
½ cup extra-virgin olive oil
2 tbsp tarragon, minced
1 tbsp thyme, minced
1 tbsp rosemary, minced
2 garlic cloves, minced
1 tsp cumin
1½ lb boneless leg of lamb, cut into 1-inch cubes
Salt and pepper

···········{Tip}···········
To skewer lamb cubes on rosemary branches, poke them first with a metal skewer.

Lamb Skewers
with Mint Chutney

I'm still surprised when I hear friends say they're not keen on lamb. I think it's probably because they've never prepared it themselves. To change their minds, I feed them these flavorful, herbal kebabs paired with a side of minty chutney. This dish is definitely a favorite at my house. *Serves 4*

1. Soak skewers in water about 30 minutes.

2. Make the chutney: Place mint, cilantro, onion, yogurt, and lemon juice in a food processor with 2 tablespoons water and process until almost smooth. Season with salt and pepper to taste. Transfer to a bowl and set aside.

3. Preheat grill or grill pan to medium-high and brush with vegetable oil.

4. Whisk olive oil, tarragon, thyme, rosemary, garlic, and cumin in a large bowl. Add lamb and toss until well coated.

5. Thread lamb onto skewers and season with salt and pepper to taste. Grill 5 to 6 minutes on each side. Let cool a few minutes before serving with mint chutney.

Ingredients

12 bamboo skewers

Cucumber Yogurt Sauce

⅓ cucumber, peeled and diced

¾ cup Greek yogurt

2 tbsp mint, minced

2 tbsp fresh lemon juice

2 tbsp sour cream

2 tbsp honey

½ tsp cumin

¼ tsp sweet paprika

Salt and pepper

1½ lb lamb loin, trimmed and cut into 1-inch cubes

2 tbsp oregano, minced

2 tsp thyme, minced

1 shallot, minced

Zest and juice of 1 lemon

2 garlic cloves, minced

¼ cup plus 2 tbsp extra-virgin olive oil

½ red onion, cut into 1-inch pieces

1 green bell pepper, cut into 1-inch pieces

1 cup cherry tomatoes

Salt and pepper

Lamb Souvlaki
with Cucumber Yogurt Sauce

I love the fact that so many cultures grill food on sticks and skewers. I've always been a fan of lamb, and this icon of Greek cooking has been a favorite of mine since I was a kid. Although it's delicious straight from the skewer, you can always remove the tender chunks of lamb after cooking for pitas and salads. *Serves 4*

1. Soak skewers in water about 30 minutes.

2. Make the cucumber yogurt sauce: Place cucumbers, yogurt, mint, lemon juice, sour cream, honey, cumin, and paprika in a small bowl and whisk. Season with salt and pepper to taste. Cover and refrigerate 30 minutes.

3. Place lamb in a large bowl. Whisk oregano, thyme, shallot, lemon zest and juice, garlic, and oil in a small bowl. Pour half of mixture over lamb and toss to coat. Cover, refrigerate, and let marinate at least 30 minutes.

4. Place onions, bell peppers, and tomatoes in another bowl; add remaining half of mixture and toss gently. Cover, refrigerate, and let marinate at least 30 minutes.

5. Thread lamb and vegetables onto skewers, varying the combinations, until all meat and vegetables have been used.

6. Heat grill or grill pan to medium-high and brush with oil. Grill lamb and vegetable skewers 5 to 7 minutes on each side. Season with salt and pepper to taste. Serve with cucumber yogurt sauce.

8 (4-inch) bamboo skewers

Fresh Tomato Salsa

4 Roma tomatoes, quartered

1/2 cup yellow onion, chopped

1 jalapeño, roughly chopped

1 garlic clove

2 tbsp cilantro, roughly chopped

1 tbsp canola oil

Salt

Potato Filling

3 medium russet potatoes, peeled
and cut into 3/4-inch cubes

2 tsp vegetable oil

1/4 lb beef chorizo

1/3 cup Monterey Jack cheese,
cut into 1/4-inch cubes

Masa

2 cups maseca

1 tsp salt

3 qt vegetable oil

2 tbsp minced cilantro

2 tbsp crumbled cotija cheese

............{Tip}............

Maseca is corn flour that's been
treated with lime.

Molotes

with Fresh Tomato Salsa

This Oaxacan street food consists of a filling that's wrapped in corn masa and fried. I probably don't need to tell you how heavenly that is, do I? In my version, chorizo, potatoes, and masa make their way onto a stick. It's the perfect party food! *Serves 4 to 6*

1. Make the salsa: Place tomatoes, onion, jalapeño, garlic, and 2 tablespoons water in a blender and blend until smooth. Strain through a sieve.

2. Pour oil into a medium saucepan over medium-high heat. Add tomato mixture and simmer about 5 minutes, or until slightly reduced and thickened. Season with salt. Let cool to room temperature, then refrigerate until ready to serve.

3. Make the filling: Place potatoes in a large pot and cover completely with water. Season with a pinch of salt. Over high heat, bring to a boil and cook until tender, about 10 minutes. Drain and transfer to a mixing bowl.

4. In a small skillet over medium-high heat, warm vegetable oil. Sauté chorizo 3 to 5 minutes, or until browned, stirring and breaking into pieces. Gently fold chorizo into potatoes. Stir in cheese until just combined. Form mixture into 8 equal balls. Place on a parchment-lined baking sheet and refrigerate at least 30 minutes.

5. Make the masa: Combine maseca, 1¾ cups water, and salt in a large mixing bowl and mix to form a ball. If it's dry and crumbly, add more water. Divide into 8 portions and flatten each into a disc large enough to wrap around 1 potato ball.

6. Fill a large, heavy pot with vegetable oil and heat to 365°F. Fry molotes, 2 at a time, 4 to 6 minutes, or until a light golden brown. Drain on paper towels and insert sticks. Top with cilantro and cotija cheese and serve with salsa.

Panzanella

with Sherry Vinaigrette

12 cocktail picks

1 loaf French bread, cut into 24 (1-inch) cubes

2 tbsp extra-virgin olive oil

1 tsp garlic powder

½ tsp salt

Pinch black pepper

Sherry Vinaigrette

¼ cup sherry vinegar

¾ cup extra virgin olive oil

½ shallot, finely chopped

1½ tsp stone-ground mustard

Sea salt

24 cherry tomatoes

24 small fresh mozzarella balls (*ciliegine*)

24 basil leaves

Panzanella, Italian bread salad, is a perfect candidate for a stick makeover. I refuse to host any type of summer outdoor party without these. They're easy to make ahead, require minimal fuss, and always disappear when served on a big platter. Sprinkle with sherry vinaigrette right before serving, and be generous! *Serves 4*

1. Preheat oven to 350°F.

2. Toss bread with oil, garlic powder, salt, and pepper. Spread pieces in a single layer on a baking sheet and bake 10 minutes, turning them halfway through cooking time.

3. Make the vinaigrette: Whisk all ingredients in a small bowl until fully incorporated. Season with salt as needed.

4. Thread 2 pieces of bread, 2 tomatoes, 2 mozzarella balls, and 2 basil leaves onto each cocktail pick. Just before serving, drizzle liberally with sherry vinaigrette.

Pinchos de Gambas

8 bamboo skewers

2 tbsp smoked paprika

2 tbsp sweet paprika

½ tbsp cumin

2 garlic cloves, minced

1 tsp salt

½ tsp pepper

2 tbsp fresh lime juice

⅓ cup plus 2 tbsp extra-virgin
olive oil, divided

1 lb tiger shrimp, cleaned and
peeled, with tails intact

These Spanish-style shrimp bites are so easy to prepare, yet so big on flavor. Smoked paprika (available in specialty food and spice stores as well as online) is not your everyday variety, so no substitutions allowed! Enjoy these with a glass of Spanish red and plenty of friends. *Serves 4*

1. Soak skewers in water 30 minutes.

2. Whisk smoked paprika, sweet paprika, cumin, garlic, salt, pepper, lime juice, and ⅓ cup of the olive oil in a medium bowl. Add shrimp and gently toss. Refrigerate 30 minutes to 1 hour.

3. Heat grill or grill pan to medium-high and brush with the remaining 2 tablespoons oil. Thread 3 shrimp per skewer and grill 3 to 4 minutes on each side, or just until shrimp has cooked through. (Be careful not to overcook.) Serve hot.

Pizza Skewers
with Garlic Butter Dipping Sauce

8 pop sticks

½ cup all-purpose flour

1 (13.8 oz) can refrigerated pizza dough

1 cup plus 2 tbsp store-bought pizza sauce, divided

2 cups grated mozzarella cheese, divided

1 cup toppings of your choice (optional), such as diced green bell peppers, diced yellow onions, cooked and crumbled Italian sausage, sliced black olives, or sliced button mushrooms

Garlic Butter Dipping Sauce

2 cups (8 sticks) butter

¼ cup minced garlic

I instantly revert to childhood when I eat these skewered pizzas, and I'm totally cool with that. They're fun, different, and delicious. Plunking each bite in the garlicky butter sauce is sheer heaven, but I must confess: I always sneak a small bowl of ranch dressing for dipping, too. *Serves 4*

1. Preheat oven to 425°F. Lightly grease a nonstick baking sheet.

2. On a clean work surface dusted with flour, roll dough into a 12-inch square, roughly ½ inch thick. (Flour as needed to prevent sticking.)

3. Spread 1 cup of the pizza sauce over dough and top with 1½ cups of the cheese and half of the additional toppings (if using).

4. Carefully roll dough and toppings from one end to the other, forming a log. Cut log into 8 equal (1-inch) rounds and place on the prepared baking sheet. Bake 12 minutes.

5. While rounds are baking, toss remaining sauce, cheese, and toppings (if using) in a bowl.

6. Remove rounds from oven and top each with a small amount of cheese mixture. Bake an additional 5 minutes, or until cheese is golden.

7. Make the sauce: Melt butter in a small saucepan over low heat. Strain through a mesh sieve into a bowl, discarding the solids. Place remaining drawn butter and garlic in a small saucepan and simmer over medium-low heat 20 minutes.

8. Thread rounds onto skewers and serve warm, with garlic butter dippng sauce.

Potato Chips on a Stick

with Spicy Ketchup

4 wooden skewers

1 qt vegetable oil

1 Yukon gold potato, sliced into paper-thin rounds

¼ cup grated Parmesan cheese

Salt and pepper

Potato chips don't always have to be an overly salty, greasy affair plucked from a nondescript foil bag. Making them at home allows you to control the flavor, and cooking them on sticks makes them fun (and not so messy). When set upright in small cups, these are great for parties: delicious and eye-catching! *Serves 4*

1. Preheat oil in a large pot over medium-high heat.

2. Thread potato slices onto skewers.

3. Once oil reaches 350°F, carefully place skewers in pot, 2 at a time, and fry 6 to 8 minutes. Drain on paper towels, sprinkle with Parmesan, and season with salt and pepper to taste. Serve warm.

{For ketchup with a kick, mix in a few dashes of Tabasco sauce.}

·············{Tip}·············
You can use a mandolin to slice potatoes paper-thin in no time.

Red Curry Shrimp and Pineapple Skewers

8 bamboo skewers

Red Curry Marinade
1 (14-ounce) can coconut milk
¼ cup Thai basil, chopped
3 tbsp red curry paste
2 tbsp cilantro, chopped
1 shallot, minced
1 garlic clove, minced
Zest and juice of 1 lime
Salt and pepper

1½ lb tiger shrimp, peeled, cleaned, and deveined, with tails intact
1 small pineapple, peeled and cut into 1-inch cubes
2 tbsp extra-virgin olive oil
Salt and pepper

Coconut, pineapple, and lime get swirled with the zesty flavors of curry, garlic, and cilantro in this recipe. I love the combination of flavors on these skewers and usually serve them with white or brown rice. They cook quickly too, making them perfect for outdoor gatherings—but remember not to overcook the shrimp! *Serves 4*

1. Soak skewers in water about 30 minutes.

2. Place all marinade ingredients in a bowl and whisk together. Add shrimp and pineapple and toss gently. Cover with plastic wrap and refrigerate 30 minutes.

3. Thread shrimp and pineapple cubes onto skewers, alternating items, until all pieces are used.

4. Heat grill or grill pan to medium-high and brush with oil. Grill skewers on each side 4 to 6 minutes, or until shrimp is just cooked through. Season lightly with salt and pepper and serve.

Savory Tofu Dango

8 wooden skewers

3 qt vegetable oil

1 cup rice flour

8 ounces silken tofu

Spicy Garlic Soy Sauce

1/2 cup soy sauce

3 tbsp mirin

1/3 cup sugar

3 tbsp minced garlic

1 tbsp Korean chili powder
(*gochugaru*)

............{Tip}............
Mirin is a sweet rice wine. In a
pinch you can substitute any
sweet white cooking wine.

This savory version of tofu dango, Japanese dumplings that are traditionally sweet, gets a dunk in spicy garlic soy sauce just before eating. It's delicious and provides a wonderful contrast to the smooth, almost nutty flavor of fried tofu. *Serves 4*

1. Preheat oil in a large, heavy pot over medium-high heat. Bring 5 quarts water to boil.

2. Place rice flour and tofu in a large bowl and knead until a smooth dough forms; if mixture is too dry, add water, 1 tablespoon at a time, until smooth. Roll into balls to make about 24 dumplings.

3. Prepare a bowl of ice water. Drop dumplings into boiling water and cook 2 to 3 minutes. Use a slotted spoon to transfer dumplings to ice water to stop the cooking process.

4. Make the garlic soy sauce: Stir soy sauce, mirin, sugar, and garlic in a small pot and simmer 10 minutes. Stir in chili powder, remove from heat, and set aside.

5. Once oil reaches 365°F, thread 3 dumplings onto each skewer. Place carefully in pot and fry 4 to 6 minutes, or until light golden brown. Drain on paper towels and brush with garlic soy sauce. Serve warm, with extra sauce for dipping.

Scotch Eggs

12 cocktail forks

1 qt vegetable oil

1 cup seasoned bread crumbs

½ cup grated Parmesan cheese

12 quail eggs, hard-boiled and peeled

½ lb low-sodium breakfast sausage, casing removed

Salt and pepper

This recipe on a stick is a riff on the British dish of hard-boiled eggs that are wrapped in sausage and bread crumbs and then deep-fried. In this version, I've used small quail eggs because, well, just look at them! They're cute and small, and when skewered they elicit that ooh-and-ahh factor we all secretly crave (right?). Best part: Their mini size makes them easier to eat. *Serves 4*

1. Preheat oil in a large, heavy pot over medium-high heat. Combine bread crumbs and Parmesan in a shallow dish; set aside.

2. Wrap each egg in 1 tablespoon sausage, using your hands to form a thin, even layer of meat around the egg. Gently roll eggs in bread-crumb mixture until fully coated.

3. Once oil reaches 350°F, carefully place eggs in pot, in 2 batches, and fry 5 minutes per batch. Drain on paper towels and season with salt and pepper to taste. Serve warm on cocktail picks.

{Quail eggs make bite-size Scotch eggs.}

Shrimp and Vegetable Tempura

8 bamboo skewers

5 cups vegetable oil

Tempura Batter

2 eggs

2 cups all-purpose flour

1 tsp salt

16 tiger shrimp, peeled and deveined

16 green beans, trimmed

2 small yams, roasted, peeled, and each cut into 4 wedges

Salt and pepper

Succulent shrimp and fresh vegetables meet ever-so-light tempura batter in these crunchy sticks. If peeling and deveining fresh shrimp isn't your thing, you can purchase them already prepared, or ask your fishmonger to do it for you. *Serves 4*

1. Soak skewers in water about 30 minutes.

2. Preheat oil in a large, heavy pot over medium-high heat.

3. Make the tempura batter: Beat eggs lightly in a bowl. Add 2 cups ice water and continue whisking. Add flour and salt and whisk until just blended. Set aside.

4. Thread 2 pieces of shrimp, 2 green beans, and 1 yam wedge onto each skewer. When oil reaches 350°F, dip each skewer into batter and gently place in pot. Fry in batches 6 to 8 minutes, or until lightly golden. Drain on paper towels, season with salt and pepper to taste, and serve hot.

Son-in-Law Eggs
with Tamarind Sauce

4 bamboo skewers

5 qt plus ⅓ cup vegetable oil, divided

8 peeled hard-boiled eggs

3 shallots, thinly sliced

4 garlic cloves, thinly sliced

Tamarind Sauce

1 cup tamarind pulp and seeds

⅔ cup honey

2 tbsp fish sauce

1 garlic clove, minced

1 tbsp chili paste

1 tsp salt

4 leaves butter lettuce

This food on a stick is based on the Thai fried egg salad of the same name. If you haven't tried it before, don't wait any longer: It's a unique treat. Deep-frying the entire egg gives it a delectable crispiness, and the tamarind sauce provides a nice, tangy contrast. I'm not sure where the name of this dish originated (legends abound), but I do know it tastes delicious! *Serves 4*

1. Preheat 5 quarts of the oil in a large pot over medium-high heat.

2. Thread eggs, 2 to a skewer; set aside.

3. Place the remaining ⅓ cup of oil in a small skillet over medium heat. Add shallots and garlic and cook, stirring occasionally, until light brown and crispy, 6 to 8 minutes. Transfer to a paper towel and set aside.

4. Make the sauce: Place tamarind and ⅔ cup boiling water in a small bowl and stir until a rough paste forms. Press paste through a fine sieve into a small saucepan over medium heat. Add honey, fish sauce, garlic, chili paste, and salt and reduce, stirring occasionally, about 6 minutes. When sauce has thickened, remove from heat and let cool. Strain into a small bowl and set aside.

5. Once oil reaches 375°F, carefully place skewers in pot, one at a time, and fry 4 to 5 minutes, or until golden. Drain on paper towels.

6. Place 2 eggs on top of each lettuce leaf. Top with fried shallots and garlic chips and drizzle with tamarind sauce.

Spaghetti and Meatballs

8 pop sticks

Homemade Meatballs
1/2 lb lean ground beef
2 tbsp minced yellow onion
1 garlic clove, minced
1 egg white
2 tbsp seasoned bread crumbs
Salt and pepper, to taste

5 cups plus 3 tbsp vegetable oil,
   divided
1/2 lb cooked spaghetti
2 cups marinara sauce
1 cup grated Parmesan cheese
Salt and pepper

I know what you're thinking: Spaghetti and meatballs on a stick? What was wrong with them on a plate? Well, you can relax. This recipe takes everyone's favorite, pops it on a stick, fries it, and increases the fun factor by about a million. Seriously. *Serves 4*

1. Line a baking sheet and a shallow baking dish with parchment paper.

2. Make the meatballs: Place all meatball ingredients in a medium bowl and mix until well combined. Shape into 1-inch balls and place on the prepared baking sheet.

3. Warm 3 tablespoons of the vegetable oil in a large skillet over medium-high heat. Add meatballs and cook, turning to brown all sides, until just cooked through. Remove from heat and let cool.

4. Gently toss meatballs, spaghetti, marinara sauce, and Parmesan in a large bowl until thoroughly combined. Place mixture in the prepared baking dish, cover, and refrigerate at least 12 hours or up to overnight.

5. Preheat the remaining 5 cups of oil to 350°F. Cut chilled pasta mixture into 8 equal squares. Remove squares from baking dish and insert a pop stick into each. Carefully place spaghetti sticks in pot, one at a time, and fry about 6 to 8 minutes, or until golden and crispy. Drain on paper towels, season with salt and pepper to taste, and serve warm.

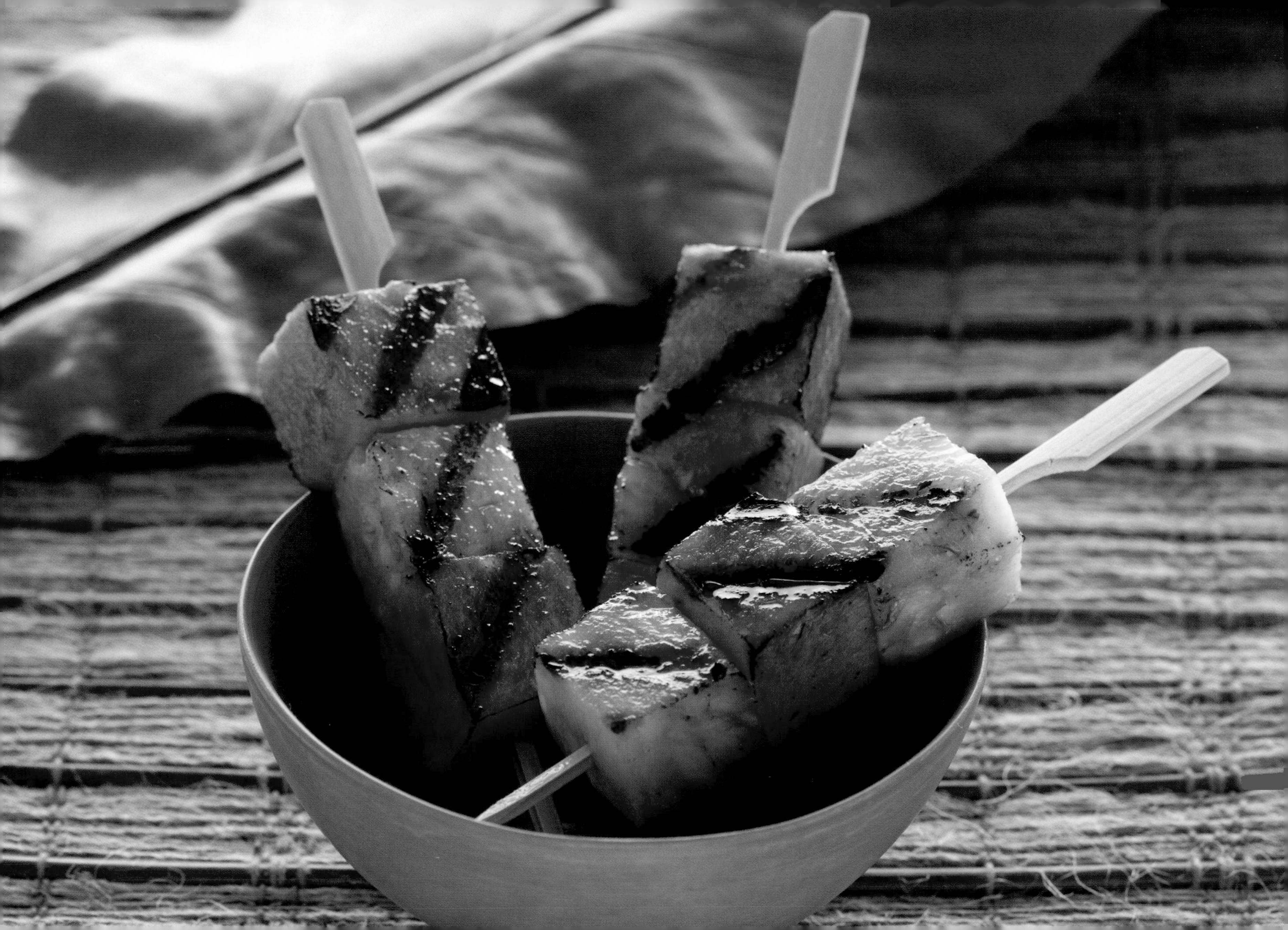

Spam and Pineapple Skewers

4 wooden skewers

2 tbsp vegetable oil

2 (12-ounce) cans Spam, cut into 2-inch cubes

2 cups fresh pineapple cubes (roughly the same size as Spam cubes)

$3/4$ cup low-sodium soy sauce

$1/4$ cup pineapple juice

$1/2$ cup light brown sugar

$1/4$ cup sugar

1 tbsp peeled and minced ginger

2 scallions, thinly sliced

If you're the type who has an aversion to Spam, then please close this book and visit a park or fly a kite. This recipe is not for you. However, if you crave the salty, robust flavor of spiced ham from a can, then let's be friends! This recipe takes island favorites and puts them on a stick—a marriage made in heaven. I'll be happy to make these for you if you ever visit, and I'll even play my ukulele. *Serves 4*

1. Soak skewers in water about 30 minutes. Preheat grill or grill pan to medium and brush with oil.

2. Thread alternating Spam and pineapple cubes onto skewers. Set aside.

3. Combine soy sauce, pineapple juice, sugars, and ginger in a small saucepan; stir. Simmer over medium heat, stirring occasionally, 15 minutes, or until mixture thickens into a glaze. Let cool and then stir in scallions.

4. Grill skewers 6 minutes per side. Brush skewers on both sides with glaze and grill an additional 2 minutes, turning over once. Serve warm.

4 wooden skewers

1 qt vegetable oil

Cajun Marinade

1/4 cup extra-virgin olive oil

2 tbsp Cajun seasoning

1 tsp black pepper

Hush Puppy Batter

1 cup self-rising cornmeal

1/2 cup self-rising flour

1 tbsp sugar

1 tsp salt

1/2 tsp black pepper

1 egg

2/3 cup buttermilk

1 scallion, thinly sliced

Spicy Buffalo Dipping Sauce

1 cup hot sauce

1/2 cup (1 stick) butter, melted

8 tiger shrimp, peeled and
    cleaned with tails intact

8 okra pods

1 andouille sausage, sliced

4 small red potatoes, boiled

2 tbsp extra-virgin olive oil

Spicy Cajun Skewers
with Spicy Buffalo Dipping Sauce

Me and my bright ideas. I wanted something Cajun inspired, but my first attempts at gumbo on a stick weren't successful. Instead, I've taken the spirit of Louisiana gumbo and reinterpreted that classic stew as a spicy, crisp-fried skewer. Make sure to have plenty of icy beer on hand for these, and—whatever you do—don't forget the hot sauce! *Serves 4*

1. Preheat vegetable oil in a large pot over medium-high heat. Soak skewers in water about 30 minutes.

2. Combine marinade ingredients in a small bowl; set aside.

3. Make the hush puppy batter: Whisk cornmeal, flour, sugar, salt, pepper, egg, buttermilk, and scallions in a large bowl; batter should be thick.

4. Once oil reaches 350°F, carefully drop large (2-ounce) spoonfuls of batter into pot and fry about 5 minutes. (Work in batches.) Drain hush puppies on paper towels and season with additional salt and pepper to taste.

5. Make the sauce: While hush puppies are draining, whisk hot sauce and butter in a small bowl.

6. Slide 1 hush puppy onto a skewer, followed by 1 shrimp, 1 okra pod, 1 slice sausage, 1 potato, another piece of shrimp, and another hush puppy; repeat with remaining skewers and ingredients. Brush liberally with Cajun marinade.

7. Heat grill or grill pan to medium-high and brush with olive oil. Grill skewers 4 to 5 minutes per side. Serve warm, accompanied by dipping sauce.

Stuffed Olives

16 cocktail picks
1½ cups kalamata olives, pitted
1 cup pistachios, shelled
½ cup goat cheese, softened
1½ cups green olives, pitted

Wonderful in cocktails or as part of an appetizer spread, these nibbles require no cooking and are a cinch to prepare. Feel free to experiment with different types of olives, just make sure they are large enough to stuff. *Serves 4*

1. Stuff each kalamata olive with a pistachio.

2. Fill a corner of a plastic sandwich bag with goat cheese and twist closed. Cut off just the tip of the corner of the bag, creating a tiny opening. Squeeze a little cheese into each green olive.

3. Thread each stuffed olive onto a cocktail pick. Enjoy!

{Try stuffing olives with garlic cloves, hard or soft cheeses, or cubes of salami.}

Suppli

16 cocktail picks

Homemade Risotto
3 to 4 cups low-sodium chicken stock
3 tbsp extra-virgin olive oil
1 shallot, minced
1 garlic clove, minced
1 cup arborio rice
½ cup dry white wine

2 tbsp unsalted butter
¾ cup grated Parmesan cheese, divided
Salt and pepper
5 cups vegetable oil
4 ounces part-skim mozzarella, cut into ¾-inch cubes
1 cup all-purpose flour
2 eggs, beaten
1 cup panko bread crumbs

God bless Italy. Any country that takes rice, wraps it around cheese, and bakes or fries it into little golden crunch balls of heaven is fine by me! Though this recipe includes instructions for homemade risotto, it's also a great way to use up restaurant risotto left over from last night. (Note: These disappear quickly. You've been warned.) *Serves 4*

1. Place chicken stock in a saucepan over low heat. Lightly grease a baking sheet.

2. Warm olive oil in a skillet over medium-high heat. Add shallots and garlic and cook, stirring occasionally, about 5 minutes. Add rice and cook another 5 minutes. Deglaze pan.

3. Lower heat to medium. Add a ladleful of stock and stir until absorbed. Continue stirring and adding stock, a ladleful at a time, until rice becomes soft but retains a little bite.

4. Remove from heat, gently stir in butter and ¼ cup of the Parmesan, and season with salt and pepper. Spread onto the prepared baking sheet and refrigerate 4 to 6 hours.

5. Once risotto is chilled, line a baking sheet with parchment paper. Heat vegetable oil to 350°F.

6. Shape a small amount of risotto into a ball. Press a piece of mozzarella into the center and cover with risotto. Place on prepared baking sheet. Repeat.

7. Place flour and eggs in separate dishes. In a third, combine panko and the remaining ½ cup of Parmesan. Lightly coat each ball in flour, shake off excess, then dip in eggs and dredge in panko mixture.

8. Fry in batches 5 to 6 minutes, or until golden. Drain on paper towels, season with salt and pepper, and serve on cocktail picks.

Sweet Potato Wedges
with Cilantro Yogurt Dipping Sauce

4 bamboo skewers

4 tbsp extra-virgin olive oil, divided

Cilantro Yogurt Dipping Sauce

1 cup Greek yogurt

3 tbsp cilantro, minced

1 tbsp mint, minced

Zest and juice of 1 lime

2 tsp honey

¼ tsp salt

1 tsp curry powder

¼ tsp cayenne pepper

Salt and pepper

2 medium red-skinned sweet potatoes (yams), each boiled and cut lengthwise into 6 wedges

This is one of my favorite ways to enjoy sweet potatoes: skewered and grilled. They're simple to prepare, and the cool, creamy dipping sauce takes only a few minutes to whip up. Pair these skewers with any smoky, grilled meat and prepare to swoon. *Serves 4*

1. Soak skewers in water about 30 minutes. Preheat grill or grill pan to medium-high and brush with half the olive oil.

2. Make the yogurt sauce: Whisk all ingredients in a small bowl until thoroughly combined. Set aside.

3. In a large bowl, whisk curry powder, cayenne pepper, and the remaining 2 tablespoons of olive oil; season with salt and pepper to taste. Add sweet potato wedges and toss to coat.

4. Pierce 3 wedges onto each skewer and grill 4 to 5 minutes per side. Remove from heat and season with salt and pepper. Serve with cilantro yogurt sauce.

Tofu Tod

with Sweet Chili Sauce

4 wooden skewers

Sweet Chili Sauce
½ cup rice wine vinegar
½ cup sugar
2 tbsp hot chili paste
1 tbsp minced garlic
1 tbsp cornstarch
2 dashes fish sauce
1 tbsp cilantro, minced

1 qt vegetable oil
6 ounces firm tofu, cut into
   1-inch pieces
Salt and pepper

Miracles happen when you fry tofu: The tender pieces gain a crunchy exterior while the interiors remain soft and cushy. I love serving these tasty little bites with a sweet chili sauce and a sprinkling of chopped peanuts for an elegant, vegetarian-friendly appetizer. *Serves 4*

1. Make the sauce: Place vinegar and sugar in a small saucepan and simmer over medium heat until sugar dissolves. Stir in chili paste and garlic. In a separate bowl, stir 3 tablespoons cold water and cornstarch. Add to vinegar mixture and whisk until sauce thickens, about 3 to 4 minutes. Remove from heat and let cool. Stir in fish sauce and cilantro. Cover and refrigerate at least 1 hour.

2. Preheat oil in a large, heavy pot over medium-high heat. Thread 3 tofu wedges onto each skewer.

3. Once oil reaches 375°F, carefully place skewers in pot and fry 8 minutes, or until golden. Drain on paper towels and season with salt and pepper to taste. Serve warm, with sweet chili sauce on the side.

Tornado Potato Sticks

4 wooden skewers
1 qt vegetable oil
2 Kennebec potatoes
1/2 cup grated Parmesan cheese
Salt and pepper

If you've visited a state fair lately, I'm sure you've seen this amazing phenomenon: long spiraling coils of golden potato twirls that look more like party decorations than anything edible. But man, oh, man—one bite and you'll realize how fantastic they are. This homemade version requires a spiral slicer and plenty of salt, pepper, and grated Parmesan. *Serves 4*

1. Preheat oil in a large, heavy pot over medium-high heat.

2. Using a spiral slicer, cut each potato into a long ribbon. Slice each spiral in half and coil each piece onto a wooden skewer.

3. Once oil reaches 350°F, carefully place skewers, 2 at a time, in pot and fry 8 to 10 minutes. Drain on paper towels and season with Parmesan and salt and pepper to taste. Serve warm.

Yakitori

8 wooden skewers

³/₄ cup soy sauce

2 tsp sesame oil

¹/₄ cup sugar

3 tbsp mirin

2 tbsp sake

1¹/₂ lb boneless skinless chicken thighs, cut into 1-inch cubes

3 leeks (white part only), thinly sliced

2 tbsp vegetable oil

1 tsp toasted sesame seeds

Bite-size pieces of tender chicken and leeks are skewered and sprinkled with sesame seeds to create this Japanese classic. *Serves 4*

1. Soak skewers in water about 30 minutes.

2. Place soy sauce, sugar, sesame oil, mirin, and sake in a small saucepan and simmer over low heat until sugar dissolves, 2 to 4 minutes. Remove from heat, stir, and let cool.

3. Pour mixture over chicken and fold together. Cover, refrigerate, and marinate 30 minutes.

4. Preheat grill or grill pan to high and brush with vegetable oil. Thread chicken and leeks onto skewers, alternating items. Grill 5 to 6 minutes per side. Sprinkle with sesame seeds and serve warm.

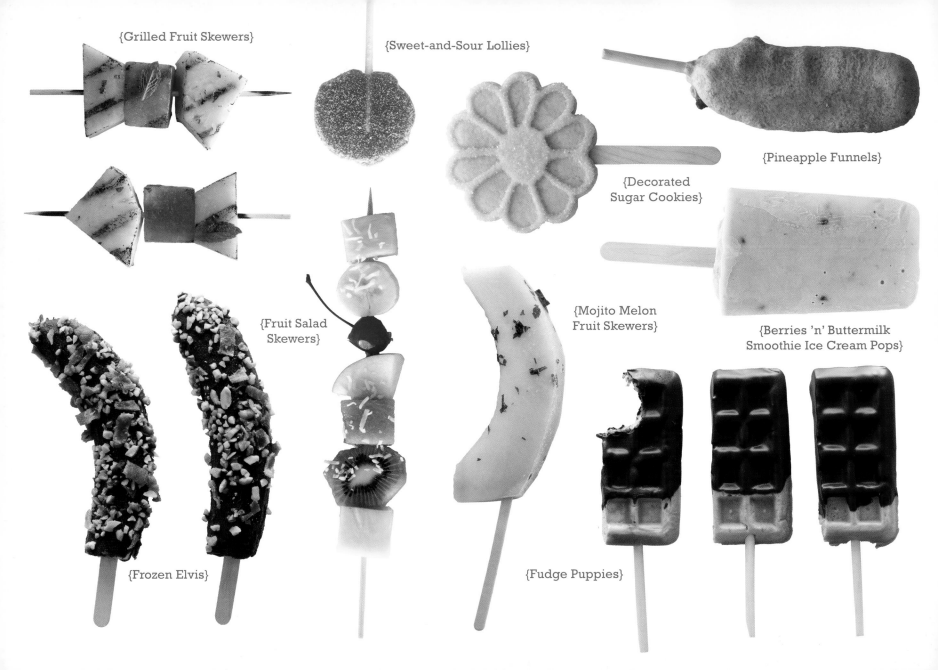

{Grilled Fruit Skewers}

{Sweet-and-Sour Lollies}

{Pineapple Funnels}

{Decorated Sugar Cookies}

{Fruit Salad Skewers}

{Mojito Melon Fruit Skewers}

{Berries 'n' Buttermilk Smoothie Ice Cream Pops}

{Frozen Elvis}

{Fudge Puppies}

Sweet Foods on a Stick

Berries 'n' Buttermilk Smoothie Ice Cream Pops

4 pop sticks

1¼ lb frozen berries, like strawberry and blueberry, or fruit,
like peach and mango

1 small banana

1 cup low-fat buttermilk

1 cup fat-free vanilla yogurt

2 tbsp honey

Sweet, simple, and with a tang of buttermilk, these smooth ice cream pops are fun to make. Feel free to use any variety of frozen fruit that you have on hand. *Serves 4*

1. Place all ingredients in a blender and blend until smooth. Pour mixture into ice-pop molds, cover with plastic wrap, and freeze 30 to 45 minutes, or until mixture begins to firm but is still soft.

2. Uncover molds and insert 1 stick into each semifrozen pop. Return to freezer at least another 2 hours, or until completely frozen.

3. Remove ice pops from molds and serve.

Cake Pops

dipped in Chocolate and Toppings

I hope you make these treats for a party or special event. Why? Because you will instantly be loved and showered with adoration. Then again, it's hard not to be when you're serving adorable little balls of cake—and on sticks, no less. *Serves 4*

12 lollipop sticks

Devil's Food Cake
1¾ cups cake flour
¾ cup cocoa powder
2 tsp baking soda
½ tsp salt
2 cups sugar
3 eggs
⅔ cup semisweet chocolate chips, melted
1¾ cups vegetable oil
1¼ cups buttermilk
¾ cup brewed coffee

1 cup store-bought cream cheese frosting

About 2 cups white chocolate melts or dark chocolate chips

············{Tip}············
It's fun to let guests dip cake pops into colorful sprinkles and other frostings and toppings.

1. Preheat oven to 350°F. Grease 2 9-inch cake pans.

2. Sift flour, cocoa powder, baking soda, and salt into a mixing bowl; set aside. In a separate bowl, whisk sugar and eggs until light and aerated. Stir in melted chocolate, vegetable oil, buttermilk, and coffee and whisk until combined.

3. In three additions, pour wet mixture into dry mixture, whisking well after each addition. Pour batter into prepared pans and bake 45 minutes to 1 hour, or until a wooden toothpick inserted in the center comes out clean.

4. Let cakes cool and then crumble into a bowl. Stir in frosting until well combined. Refrigerate mixture 15 minutes.

5. Line a baking sheet with parchment paper. Remove cake mixture from refrigerator and form into 1½-inch balls, setting each on baking sheet. (You should have 12 cake balls.) Pierce the top of each with a lollipop stick and refrigerate another 15 minutes.

6. While cake balls chill, melt chocolate in a double boiler, stirring gently until smooth. Dip each cake ball in melted white chocolate and allow excess to drip off. Let set a few minutes before dipping in sprinkles or other toppings and serving.

Candy Apples

4 thick wooden sticks

4 Granny Smith apples

1½ cups sugar

¼ cup light corn syrup

¼ tsp ground cinnamon

7 to 8 drops red food coloring

Images of golden sunlight and cooler nights fill my mind when I think of these sugary coated treats. Crunchy candy on the outside hides the Granny Smith's tart interior. It's the perfect autumn snack. *Serves 4*

1. Grease a baking sheet. Pierce the top of each apple with a wooden stick.

2. Bring sugar, corn syrup, and ½ cup water to a boil in a small saucepan. Once mixture has reached 300°F (it will take about 30 to 40 minutes), add cinnamon and food coloring, stirring until mixture is smooth.

3. One at a time, carefully dip a skewered apple into sugar mixture and twirl to coat evenly. Allow excess to drip off and place, stick side up, on the prepared baking sheet. Allow to cool and harden before serving.

Caramel Apples

Rolled in Chopped Nuts

4 thick wooden sticks

1 cup light brown sugar

½ cup light corn syrup

½ cup (1 stick) salted butter

½ (14-ounce) can evaporated milk

1 tbsp vanilla extract

4 Granny Smith apples

2 cups dry-roasted peanuts
(optional), chopped

No, it wasn't the promise of dressing up as Evel Knievel or Ponch from *CHiPs* that excited me about Halloween as a child. (OK, maybe those did, too.) What I loved *most* was making caramel apples with my mother and ending up with sticky arms and matted hair by the time we were done. I've since learned how to make them a bit more efficiently, but I still dress up like Erik Estrada now and again. *Serves 4*

1. Line a baking sheet with waxed paper.

2. Combine brown sugar and corn syrup in a medium pot over medium heat and cook until mixture reaches 245°F. Stir in butter, condensed milk, and vanilla and whisk until smooth, 3 to 4 minutes.

3. Pierce each apple with a wooden stick and gently dip and roll in caramel sauce until evenly coated. Roll each apple in chopped nuts (if using) to coat. Place, stick side up, on prepared baking sheet until caramel coating hardens slightly.

..........{Tip}..........

To make Caramel Pears, replace apples with pears and chopped peanuts with chopped hazelnuts.

Caramel Popcorn Balls

8 wood sticks

1½ cups sugar

½ cup dark brown sugar

½ cup light corn syrup

2 tbsp butter

2 tsp baking soda

1½ tsp salt

8 cups popped popcorn

Nutty, fresh popcorn is introduced to sweet, sticky caramel and a tiny dash of salt in this recipe on a stick. Because the caramel keeps everything together, these travel and keep well—although I can't imagine having any leftovers. *Serves 4*

1. Combine sugars and corn syrup with ⅓ cup water in a saucepan and bring to a boil, stirring occasionally until sugars dissolve. Once mixture has reached 240°F, remove from heat and stir in butter.

2. Return to heat and continue cooking until mixture reaches 300°F. Remove from heat and carefully stir in baking soda and salt. (The mixture will bubble aggressively, so stir with caution.)

3. Place popcorn in a large bowl and gently fold in caramel mixture until well coated. Line a baking sheet with parchment paper.

4. Using greased heatproof gloves, take a handful of caramel corn and roll it into a ball. Place on the prepared baking sheet and pierce with a pop stick. Repeat to form 8 balls. Refrigerate 30 minutes to 1 hour, or until firm. Let sit at room temperature about 15 minutes before serving.

Chocolate-Covered Cheesecake

8 pop sticks

Crust
1 cup graham cracker crumbs
2 tbsp butter, melted
1 tbsp sugar

Filling
3 (8-ounce) packages cream
   cheese, softened
3/4 cup sugar
1 3/4 tbsp all-purpose flour
3 eggs
1/4 cup heavy cream
2 tbsp sour cream
2 tsp lemon zest
1 tsp vanilla extract

4 cups semisweet chocolate chips

I'll visit almost any state fair that serves cheesecake on a stick. You know why? It frees up my other hand to hold a second serving. In my version, slices of cheesecake are set on a stick and dipped in chocolate. *Serves 8*

1. Preheat oven to 350°F.

2. Make the crust: Grease an 8-inch cake pan or springform pan. Combine cracker crumbs, butter, and sugar in a small bowl and stir until well combined. Press mixture into the prepared pan. Set aside.

3. For the filling: Combine cream cheese and sugar in a bowl and beat, using an electric mixer, until smooth and fluffy. Stir in flour. Add eggs, one by one, and then cream and sour cream, stirring until well combined. Gently fold in lemon zest and vanilla and pour mixture over prepared crust.

4. Place pan in a water bath and bake 45 minutes to 1 hour, or until cheesecake has barely set.

5. Remove pan from water bath and let cool to room temperature before cutting into 8 equal slices. Slide a pop stick into bottom of each slice. Freeze at least 1 hour.

6. Line a baking sheet with parchment paper. Melt chocolate chips in a double boiler over medium-low heat. Dip cheesecake slices one by one into chocolate and gently shake off excess to create a thin, even layer of chocolate. Place on baking sheet and refrigerate at least 1 hour or until ready to serve.

Chocolate Fondue

4 fondue picks

2¹/₂ cups semisweet chocolate chips

¹/₂ recipe homemade marsh-mallows (page 161)

1 cup fresh dark sweet cherries, pitted

1 cup fresh strawberries, stems removed

1 cup caramel squares

12 mini doughnuts

8 pretzel sticks

I'm having a hard time deciding whether the corn dog or fondue is the quintessential food on a stick. You can't really eat either *without* a stick, so they'd both be worthy of the title. While I'm figuring out that conundrum, I encourage you to try this dessert fondue. Feel free to dip anything and everything in there, won't you? My favorite is pretzels, for that irresistible sweet and salty mash-up. *Serves 4*

1. Melt chocolate chips in a double boiler over medium heat, stirring occasionally. While chocolate is melting, arrange remaining ingredients on a serving platter.

2. Pour melted chocolate into a fondue pot and place over a small candle. (If using an electric fondue pot, set to low or warm heat.) Serve, stirring fondue occasionally to maintain a smooth consistency.

Chocolate-Tipped Peppermint Sticks

8 multicolored peppermint sticks

1 cup white chocolate chips

Colored sprinkles

Food on a stick is fun. Food on a *stick that you can eat* is even more fun! If you can't find peppermint sticks, just substitute any flavor of old-fashioned stick candy you like. These are great for children's parties. *Serves 4*

1. Line a baking sheet with parchment paper.

2. Melt white chocolate in a double boiler over medium heat, stirring until smooth. One at a time, dip peppermint sticks partway into white chocolate and then roll in colored sprinkles.

3. Lay sticks on prepared baking sheet and let set, about 30 minutes, before serving. Call the kids!

Cinnamon Rolls

with Creamy Vanilla Icing

12 pop sticks

1 can ready-to-bake cinnamon rolls

Creamy Vanilla Icing

1 cup (2 sticks) unsalted butter, softened

$\frac{1}{2}$ cup cream cheese, softened

3 cups powdered sugar

2 tsp vanilla extract

Pinch salt

If you're thinking, "These are just cinnamon rolls stuck with a stick," well, yes, technically, you are correct. But what you might not realize is that they're exponentially more fun when eaten vertically. And fun equals flavor—am I right? *Serves 4*

1. Prepare cinnamon rolls according to directions on package.

2. While rolls are baking, cream together butter, cream cheese, and powdered sugar until light and fluffy. Stir in vanilla and salt until fully incorporated. Set aside.

3. Transfer baked cinnamon rolls to a cooling rack and, while warm, insert a pop stick into the side of each. Spread each with a thin layer of icing and let cool.

4. Once cinnamon rolls are completely cool, spread with another layer of icing and serve.

Cocktail Cubes

20 cocktail picks

About ¹/₃ cup blackberries

About ¹/₃ cup blueberries

About ¹/₃ cup raspberries

About 2 cups all-natural fruit
juice, flavor of your choice

This is such a simple recipe: Fresh berries make their way into ice cube trays and are topped with fruit juice. The resulting colorful cocktail cubes can be dropped into any drink, whether boozy or virgin. *Serves 4*

1. Place 1 blackberry, 1 blueberry, and 1 raspberry into each section of an ice cube tray and then fill with fruit juice. Cover tray with plastic wrap; poke a cocktail pick through wrap into each section.

2. Freeze at least 2 hours and up to 24 hours.

3. Remove cubes from tray and serve in the drink of your choice. Cheers!

Decorated Sugar Cookies

with Decorating Icing

16 pop sticks

⅓ cup plus 1 tbsp unsalted butter, softened

⅔ cup and 2 tbsp sugar

1 egg

½ tsp vanilla extract

1⅓ cups all-purpose flour, plus extra for rolling

½ tsp baking powder

¼ tsp salt

Decorating Icing

2 egg whites

⅛ tsp cream of tartar

2⅔ cups powdered sugar

Food coloring in different colors

Sparkling sugar, nonpareils, or other decorations

·············{Tip}·············

Let one layer of icing set before piping on another in a different color.

Putting cookies on pop sticks adds a touch of whimsy and showcases their beautiful, hand-piped adornments. These sweet treats make wonderful gifts for parties, showers, weddings, or any occasions that you want to make special. *Serves 4*

1. Preheat oven to 400°F.

2. With an electric mixer, cream butter and granulated sugar until light and fluffy. Add egg and vanilla and continue beating until combined.

3. Sift flour, baking powder, and salt into a medium bowl. Stir flour mixture into butter mixture until well combined. Form dough into a flat disc and wrap tightly with plastic wrap. Refrigerate at least 1 hour.

4. Lightly flour a clean surface and roll out chilled dough to a thickness of ½ inch. Using cookie cutters, cut out 12 cookies and place on an ungreased cookie sheet. Bake about 6 to 8 minutes, or until edges brown lightly.

5. While cookies are baking, make the decorating icing: In the bowl of a stand mixer, whisk egg whites, cream of tartar, and 2 teaspoons water until light and frothy. Add powdered sugar, a little at a time, and continue whisking until sugar is fully incorporated and icing forms stiff peaks.

6. Transfer baked cookies to a cooling rack and, while warm, insert a pop stick in each. Allow to cool completely.

7. Add a couple drops of food coloring to a portion of the icing, using a different bowl for each color. Transfer icing to a piping bag with a small tip or to a plastic bag with the corner snipped off. Decorate cookies and let sit about 1 hour, or until icing is completely set. Serve.

Deep-Fried Candy Bars

4 pop sticks

2 cups vegetable oil

4 candy bars, such as Mars Bars, Snickers, and Milky Ways

Batter

1 cup all-purpose flour

1 cup milk

$1/2$ tbsp sugar

$1/4$ tsp baking soda

$1/4$ tsp salt

Powdered sugar for serving (optional)

Not many recipes can be described as obscene, outrageous, and indecent—this one can. You'll see these confections served at state fairs all over the place, and for that reason I'm glad state fairs are held only once a year. I'm not sure my heart could handle these on a regular basis. *Serves 4*

1. Preheat oil in a large, heavy pot over medium-high heat. Line a baking sheet with parchment paper.

2. Pierce each candy bar with a pop stick, place on the prepared baking sheet, and refrigerate 30 minutes.

3. Whisk all batter ingredients until little to no lumps remain. One at a time, dip chilled candy bars in batter and coat well.

4. Once oil reaches 390°F, carefully place candy bars in oil one at a time and fry about 3 to 4 minutes. Drain on a paper towel, sprinkle with powdered sugar if desired, and serve hot.

8 bamboo skewers

Doughnut Batter
5 qt vegetable oil
2 packets active dry yeast
3½ tbsp granulated sugar
1 egg, lightly beaten
1 tbsp vanilla extract
1 tsp ground cinnamon
¼ tsp ground nutmeg
1 tsp salt
¼ cup plus 1 tbsp butter, melted
2½ cups all-purpose flour, plus
    more for rolling

Sugar Glaze
¼ cup whole milk
2 tsp vanilla extract
2 cups powdered sugar, sifted

Decorations of your choice,
    such as shredded coconut,
    multicolored sprinkles, and
    chopped peanuts

·············{Tip}···········
This recipe makes about 32
homemade doughnut holes.

Doughnut Holes
with Sugar Glaze and Toppings

Doughnut holes on a stick mean no sugar-crusted fingers, and I appreciate that. If you're wondering if it's possible to have doughnut holes without doughnuts—well, of course it is! You could just as easily make Doughnuts on a Stick . . . but what on earth will you eat while you're making Doughnut Holes on a Stick? (See, I've totally figured it out.) *Serves 4*

1. Preheat oil in a large pot over medium-high heat.

2. Place 1 cup warm water in a bowl and sprinkle with yeast and granulated sugar. Allow mixture to bubble and then add egg, vanilla, cinnamon, nutmeg, salt, butter, and flour. Knead mixture until a smooth dough forms, about 7 minutes.

3. Place dough in a greased bowl, cover with a damp cloth, and place in a warm dry area. Let rise 30 minutes.

4. Punch down risen dough and roll out 1 inch thick on a floured surface. Using a small circle cutter, cut out holes and place them on a greased baking sheet. Cover with a damp cloth and let rise another 30 minutes.

5. Meanwhile, make the glaze: Combine milk and vanilla in a small saucepan and bring to a simmer. Remove from heat and whisk in powdered sugar until smooth. Set aside and let cool slightly.

6. Once oil reaches 365°F, carefully drop in doughnut holes, a few at a time, and fry on each side 4 to 5 minutes, or until golden brown. Drain on paper towels.

7. Dip each doughnut hole in glaze and roll in decoration of choice. Place on a cooling rack and let glaze set. Skewer each on a bamboo skewer and serve.

Fresh Mango and Chili Powder

with Lime

16 bamboo skewers

2 tbsp chili powder

1 tbsp lime zest

½ tsp salt

2 mangoes, peeled, pitted,
and sliced into 8 wedges

Juice of 1 lime

Throughout Mexico and Latin America, you'll find sweet fruit served with contrasting flavors, like salt and chili powder. These skewers are fun, healthy, and easy to eat. *Serves 4*

1. Combine chili powder, zest, and salt in a small bowl; set aside.

2. Place mango wedges and lime juice in a separate bowl and toss gently. Thread mango onto skewers. Sprinkle all over with chili mixture and serve.

Frozen Bananas

Dipped in Chocolate

4 pop sticks

4 medium bananas, peeled

4 cups semisweet chocolate chips

In a past life, I was a monkey. I'm sure of this. I think nothing of eating bananas every single day. In this classic recipe, frozen bananas get covered in semisweet chocolate and served on a stick. I like to keep a few of these in the freezer for those monkey moments in life. *Serves 4*

1. Line a baking sheet with parchment paper. Insert a pop stick into the bottom of each banana and place on prepared baking sheet. Freeze at least 1 hour.

2. Melt chocolate chips in a double boiler over medium-low heat, stirring occasionally.

3. Dip each frozen banana in melted chocolate and allow excess to drip off. Return chocolate-dipped bananas to parchment-lined baking sheet and refreeze, about 1 hour. Keep frozen until ready to serve.

············{Tip}············

Don't let a good banana go to waste! Before it's too late, just peel, dip, and freeze.

{Try adding chopped nuts.}

Frozen Elvis

4 pop sticks

4 medium bananas, peeled

1 cup chopped cooked bacon

1 cup dry-roasted peanuts, chopped

4 cups semisweet chocolate chips

It's hard to choose a favorite sandwich. When I first tasted the Elvis—peanut butter, bananas, and crispy bacon on toasty grilled bread—I knew I hit the jackpot. This recipe is a riff on that classic sandwich that makes an irresistible and easy-to-eat snack, and I dedicate it to all the bacon lovers out there. *Serves 4*

1. Line a baking sheet with parchment paper.

2. Insert a pop stick in the bottom of each banana and place on prepared baking sheet. Freeze at least 1 hour.

3. Combine bacon and peanuts in a shallow dish and set aside.

4. Melt chocolate chips in a double boiler over medium-low heat, stirring occasionally. Dip each frozen banana in melted chocolate and allow excess to drip off. Roll in bacon-peanut mixture and then return to parchment-lined baking sheet. Refreeze at least 1 hour. Keep frozen until ready to serve.

Fruit Salad Skewers

with Sweet and Fluffy Dipping Sauce

12 bamboo skewers

1 Granny Smith apple, cored and chopped into ½-inch pieces

2 kiwis, peeled and sliced into ½-inch pieces

2 mangoes, peeled, pitted, and cut into ½-inch cubes

1 banana, peeled and sliced into ½-inch pieces

1 cup pineapple cubes

1 cup seedless watermelon cubes

8 maraschino cherries

Sweet and Fluffy Dipping Sauce

1¼ cups Marshmallow Fluff

¾ cup sour cream

½ cup shredded coconut

You could say this bright, colorful, and otherwise healthy skewer is merely a vehicle for the scrumptious, gooey dipping sauce. But I'd never say that. (Wink, wink.) Perfect for kids and adults who shamelessly hide behind fruit to get to the good stuff. *Serves 4*

1. Arrange fruit pieces on skewers, varying the combinations.

2. Make the dipping sauce: Whisk Marshmallow Fluff and sour cream in a bowl until completely combined and smooth.

3. Sprinkle skewers with coconut and serve with dipping sauce.

{Cutting fruit into roughly equal-sized ½-inch pieces makes for pretty presentation and easy eating.}

Fudge Pops

4 pop sticks

⅓ cup sugar

1 tbsp cornstarch

1½ tbsp unsweetened cocoa powder

2 tbsp semisweet chocolate chips, melted

1¼ cups whole milk

½ tsp vanilla extract

½ tbsp unsalted butter

Cool and creamy, these chocolaty ice pops hit the spot on those long, hot summer nights. Make them ahead and keep a few batches on hand for when the mercury rises. *Serves 4*

1. Combine sugar, cornstarch, cocoa powder, melted chocolate, and milk in a medium saucepan over medium heat and cook, stirring frequently, until mixture thickens, about 10 minutes. Remove from heat, add vanilla and butter, and stir until well combined.

2. Let mixture cool slightly and then pour into a 4-serving ice-pop mold. Freeze 30 minutes and then insert sticks. Freeze completely before serving.

Fudge Puppies

with Chocolate and Toppings

4 wooden sticks

2 frozen Belgian waffles, toasted and cut down the middle

4 cups semisweet chocolate chips

If my pants no longer fit, then you can blame this recipe. No need to make your waffles from scratch (unless you really, really want to)—the frozen ones work just fine. Just don't cut corners on the chocolate. Make sure to use a high-quality chip. *Serves 4*

1. Insert a wooden stick into each half waffle and freeze about 30 minutes.

2. Melt chocolate chips in a double boiler over medium-low heat, stirring occasionally.

3. Line a baking sheet with parchment paper. Dip frozen waffle sticks in melted chocolate, creating a thin, even layer. Place on baking sheet and let chocolate set before serving.

{This classic fair food is as easy as 1–2–3!}

·············{Tip}·············
Before chocolate sets completely you can dip Fudge Puppies in chopped peanuts, sprinkles, or homemade whipped cream (page 174).

Grilled Fruit Skewers

with Honey-Mint Syrup

8 bamboo skewers

Honey-Mint Syrup
½ cup sugar
¼ cup honey
1 cup mint, minced
2 tbsp lime zest

1 pineapple, peeled, cored, and
    cut into 1-inch chunks
½ small seedless watermelon,
    peeled and cut into 1-inch
    chunks
½ small cantaloupe, peeled,
    seeded, and cut into 1-inch
    chunks
Salt to taste

············{Tip}············
A squeeze of lemon will preserve
the color of fresh fruit.

Grilling fruit brings out its natural sugars and imparts a touch of summer, and the honey-mint syrup makes these skewers truly special. Who says meat should get all the glory on the grill? *Serves 4*

1. Make the syrup: Bring sugar, honey, and ½ cup water to a boil in a small saucepan over medium-high heat, stirring occasionally, until sugar dissolves. Meanwhile, soak skewers in cold water 30 minutes.

2. Remove syrup from heat and let cool slightly. Stir in mint and lime zest and set aside.

3. Heat grill or grill pan to medium-high and coat with cooking spray. Thread fruit onto skewers and sprinkle with salt.

4. Grill skewers (in batches if necessary) 3 to 4 minutes per side. Brush honey-mint syrup on both sides and grill an additional 1 minute. Drizzle with more syrup and serve.

{Cut fruit is pretty and easy to eat, especially on a stick!}

Homemade Marshmallows

4 bamboo sticks

½ cup sugar

2 tsp light corn syrup

2 tbsp (2 envelopes) unflavored gelatin

1½ tsp vanilla extract

1½ egg whites

Powdered sugar, as needed

............{Tip}............
Serve with chocolate fondue
for an irresistible treat!

Handcrafted marshmallows are so much tastier than the bagged, store-bought variety. Plus they're prettier. These fluffy cubes look beautiful when skewered and will bring a smile to everyone's face. I always make extra so I can snack while assembling. *Serves 4*

1. Line a baking sheet or dish with parchment paper. Stir gelatin into ⅓ cup water.

2. Place sugar, ⅓ cup water, and corn syrup in a small saucepan over medium-high heat. Bring to a boil, stirring, and cook until sugar dissolves and temperature reaches 240°F.

3. Carefully pour sugar mixture into gelatin mixture, stirring constantly. Let sit 5 minutes.

4. Using an electric mixer, whip egg whites until soft peaks form. With mixer on medium-low speed, pour sugar–gelatin mixture into egg whites in a slow, steady stream. Continue whipping until stiff peaks form.

5. Pour mixture into 8-by-8-inch baking sheet or dish and refrigerate until stiffened, about 3 hours.

6. Turn marshmallow out onto a surface sprinkled with powdered sugar; peel off parchment. Cut into 4 cubes and insert a bamboo stick into each. Serve.

Ice Cream Sandwiches

4 pop sticks

Chocolate Chip Cookies
1 cup light brown sugar
3/4 cup sugar
2 cups all-purpose flour
1 tsp baking powder
1 tsp baking soda
1 tsp salt
2 eggs
1 cup (2 sticks) unsalted butter, softened
1 tsp vanilla extract
1 cup chocolate chips

4 cups vanilla ice cream, slightly softened

············{Tip}············
You can use almost any cookie, just make sure it's sturdy enough not to crumble.

Ice cream sandwiches were hands-down my favorite treat as a kid. Now, as an adult, I like to make them from scratch, using homemade cookies and the ice cream of my choice. And, of course, I put all that cold, sweet goodness on a stick. *Serves 4*

1. Preheat oven to 350°F. Line a baking sheet with parchment paper.

2. Make the cookies: Combine sugars, flour, baking powder, baking soda, and salt in a large bowl. In a separate bowl, use an electric mixer to beat eggs until light and fluffy; add butter and vanilla and continue beating until combined. Add dry mixture a little at a time to egg mixture, stirring with a wooden spoon. Continue stirring until ingredients are fully incorporated.

3. Drop dough by heaping spoonful (about 2½ tablespoons each) onto prepared baking sheet and bake 12 to 14 minutes. Transfer cookies to a cooling rack and let cool to room temperature.

4. Top the underside of 1 cookie with 1 cup ice cream and press a second cookie on top. Repeat with remaining cookies and ice cream. Tightly wrap each ice cream sandwich individually in plastic wrap and freeze at least 30 minutes, or until ready to serve.

Margarita Jell-O Shots

80 cocktail picks

3 (6-ounce) packages lime
    or strawberry Jell-O

1 cup tequila

2 tbsp freshly squeezed lime
    juice

2 tbsp triple sec

I know what you're thinking: "Really, Matt, Jell-O shots?" Consider it an ode to spring breaks past. And on a stick, no less. Beach and suntan lotion are optional. *Serves a party*

1. Line a 9-by-9-inch baking dish with plastic wrap.

2. Combine Jell-O powder and 2½ cups boiling water in a large bowl and stir to dissolve. Add tequila, lime juice, and triple sec and stir until well combined. Pour mixture into prepared baking dish and refrigerate at least 3 hours or up to 24 hours.

3. Once Jell-O has set completely, turn out onto a clean surface and peel off plastic wrap. Cut into 1-inch cubes and serve on cocktail picks. Cheers!

············{Tip}············
Lose the plastic cups. Cocktail picks make these jiggly cubes easier to eat.

Mojito Melon Fruit Skewers
with Mojito Mix

8 pop sticks

½ honeydew melon, cut into
    8 wedges

Mojito Mix

1 tbsp powdered sugar

Juice of 3 limes

5 sprigs mint

¾ cup white rum

Fruit on a stick is fun for the grown-up set! The minty sweet taste of a mojito makes a tasty dressing for cool honeydew melon. This recipe is a favorite at summer parties. *Serves 4*

1. Arrange melon wedges in an 8-by-8-inch baking dish.

2. Make the mojito mix: Place all ingredients plus ½ cup water in a blender and pulse until mint is finely chopped. Pour mixture over melon wedges and refrigerate 1 hour.

3. Line a baking sheet with parchment paper. Pierce each melon wedge with a pop stick and arrange in a single layer on prepared baking sheet. Freeze 20 to 30 minutes. Serve cold.

Pineapple Funnels

4 wooden sticks

1½ qt vegetable oil

Funnel Cake Batter

1½ cups milk

2 eggs

2 cups all-purpose flour

1 tbsp light brown sugar

2 tsp ground cinnamon

1 tsp baking powder

½ tsp salt

1 pineapple, peeled, cored, and cut into 4 sticks 4 inches long and 1½ inches wide

Powdered sugar, optional

How much do I love funnel cakes? Let me count the ways: I once ate four in one visit to a theme park, but I don't suggest you follow my lead. What makes me love them even more? When they surround juicy morsels of fresh pineapple and are served on sticks. Complete this over-the-top creation with a light dusting of powdered sugar . . . if you dare. *Serves 4*

1. Preheat oil in a large, heavy pot over medium-high heat.

2. Make the batter: Beat milk and eggs in a small bowl. In a separate bowl, sift flour, brown sugar, cinnamon, baking powder, and salt. Gradually add milk mixture to dry mixture, whisking until fully incorporated and no lumps remain.

3. Pierce the bottom of each pineapple piece with a stick. Pat pineapple dry with paper towels.

4. Once oil reaches 350°F, dip pineapple sticks in batter, carefully place in pot (work in batches, if necessary), and fry 5 to 6 minutes, or until golden brown. Drain on paper towels. Dust with powdered sugar, if desired, and serve hot.

Red and White Sangria Pops

24 pop sticks

Red Sangria
¾ cup red wine
1¼ cups orange juice
1 tbsp powdered sugar

White Sangria
¾ cup white wine
1 cup white grape juice
¼ cup peach nectar

24 small 3-oz cups
1 orange, thinly sliced
1 lemon, thinly sliced
1 lime, thinly sliced
2 kiwis, peeled and thinly sliced
½ cup red grapes
½ cup green grapes
½ cup strawberries, stems removed and thinly sliced

Inspired by Spanish sangria, these adult pops are fun and simple to prepare. I wouldn't be too fussy about what type of wine you use; it certainly doesn't need to be the most expensive. *Serves 8*

1. In one pitcher, combine red sangria ingredients; stir and set aside. In another pitcher, combine white sangria ingredients; stir and set aside.

2. Arrange cups on a baking sheet and place a few pieces of different fruits in each one. Fill 12 of the cups with the red wine mixture and 12 with the white wine mixture. Cover all cups with a sheet of plastic wrap. Poke a pop stick through plastic wrap into each cup.

3. Freeze cups at least 4 hours. Remove from freezer, peel cups and plastic wrap off pops, and serve.

{Cool it, baby!}

S'mores

4 cocktail picks

2 cups graham cracker crumbs

4 cups semisweet chocolate chips

4 homemade marshmallows
   (recipe on page 161)

A campground classic that you keep on the stick. If you ask me, these taste even better than the s'mores of my youth because they feature homemade marshmallows. Again, don't be cheap about the chocolate! *Serves 4*

1. Line a baking sheet with parchment paper. Place graham cracker crumbs in a shallow dish and set aside. Spear marshmallows with cocktail picks.

2. Melt chocolate chips in a double boiler over medium heat, stirring occasionally. Dip marshmallow sticks in chocolate, one at a time, and let excess drip off. Roll in graham cracker crumbs and place on prepared baking sheet. Serve immediately. Or, if you'd like the chocolate to set, refrigerate about 1 hour before serving.

{Skewer, serve, and then make s'more!}

Strawberry Shortcake
with Homemade Whipped Cream

16 small bamboo skewers

2 cups pound cake cut into 1-inch cubes (store-bought is fine)

2 cups strawberries, stems removed

Whipped Cream

1 cup heavy cream

2 tbsp sugar

2 tsp vanilla extract

This recipe is a cinch to prepare and tastes like spring on a stick. The most difficult step is making the whipped cream—and it's not difficult at all. Plus, you can reward yourself by licking the bowl and mixing spoon when you're done! *Serves 4*

1. Thread alternating pieces of pound cake and strawberries onto skewers.

2. Make whipped cream: Combine cream and sugar in a bowl. Using a hand mixer, whip until stiff peaks form. Gently fold in vanilla. Serve alongside cake and strawberry skewers.

·············{Tip}············
This homemade whipped cream is quick, easy, and oooh so delicious.

Sweet-and-Sour Lollies

These pops have a tang that might just make your mouth pucker. They also offer an unexpected touch of fizz, thanks to the baking soda. *Serves 16*

16 lollipop sticks

1½ cups sugar

¼ cup light corn syrup

½ tbsp flavored oil of your choice (strawberry, orange, grape, apple)

7 to 8 drops food coloring (color should correspond to the flavored oil)

Fizzy Dip Mix

½ cup powdered sugar

2 tbsp citric acid powder

2 tsp baking soda

·········{Tip}··········

It's fun to dip almost any candy on a stick in this sweet-and-sour mix, made with citric acid powder (available wherever canning supplies are sold). Moisture activates the fizz!

1. Place granulated sugar, corn syrup, and ½ cup water in a small saucepan and bring to a boil. Continue cooking until mixture reaches 300°F, about 30 to 40 minutes. Remove from heat, add flavored oil and food coloring, and stir until smooth.

2. Place sticks 3 inches apart on a silicone baking mat and slowly pour candy mixture over the top part of each stick. (You can also use candy molds, following the product's directions.) Let cool.

3. Make the dip: Whisk powdered sugar, citric acid, and baking soda in a small bowl. Brush lollipops lightly with water and dip into powdered sugar mixture. Serve with a small amount of powdered sugar mixture on the side for dipping. If wrapping the pops individually, include small pouches of powdered sugar mixture for later use.

{Do the dip!}

Sweet Tofu Dango

with Sesame Sugar and Sweet Soy Sauce

12 cocktail picks

Sesame Sugar
½ cup black sesame seeds, crushed
¼ cup sugar

Sweet Soy Sauce
⅔ cup sugar
1 cup low-sodium soy sauce
1 cinnamon stick
2 star anise

1½ cups rice flour
8 ounces silken tofu

These little dumplings of tofu are ever-so-slightly sweet with spice notes that include cinnamon and star anise. The addition of soy sauce gives them a unique taste, and they are delightful with tea and for those moments when you don't need to have your taste buds smacked with something overly sweet. *Serves 4*

1. Make the sesame sugar: Combine crushed sesame seeds and ¼ cup of the sugar in a small bowl; set aside.

2. Make the sweet soy sauce: Stir soy sauce, the remaining ⅔ cup sugar, cinnamon, and star anise in a small saucepan over medium heat; stirring occasionally, simmer about 20 minutes to reduce by one-third. Remove from heat and let cool; discard cinnamon stick and star anise.

3. Mix rice flour and tofu in a medium bowl, kneading until a smooth dough forms. If dough is dry, add water, a tablespoon at a time.

4. Bring a medium pot of water to a boil. Roll dough into 1-inch balls. (You should have about 12 balls.) Carefully place balls a few at a time into pot and boil 5 to 7 minutes, or until cooked through.

5. Roll half the cooked balls in sesame-seed mixture and drizzle the other half with the sweet soy sauce. Serve with cocktail picks.

Ingredient Index

Conversion Chart

Use these rounded equivalents to convert between the traditional American systems used to measure volume and weight and the metric system.

{Oven Temperatures}

	°F	°C	Gas Mark
Very cool	250–275	130–140	$^1/_2$ –2
Cool	300	148	2
Warm	325	163	3
Medium	350	177	4
Medium hot	375–400	190–204	5–6
Hot	425	218	7
Very hot	450–475	232–245	8–9

{Weights}

American/British	Metric
$^1/_4$ oz	7 g
$^1/_2$ oz	15 g
1 oz	30 g
2 oz	55 g
3 oz	85 g
4 oz ($^1/_4$ lb)	110 g
5 oz	140 g
6 oz	170 g
7 oz	200 g
8 oz ($^1/_2$ lb)	225 g
9 oz	250 g
10 oz	280 g
11 oz	310 g
12 oz ($^3/_4$ lb)	340 g
13 oz	370 g
14 oz	400 g
15 oz	425 g
16 oz (1 lb)	450 g

{Volume}

American	Imperial	Metric
$^1/_4$ tsp		1.25 ml
$^1/_2$ tsp		2.5 ml
1 tsp		5 ml
$^1/_2$ tbsp (1$^1/_2$ tsp)		7.5 ml
1 tbsp (3 tsp)		15 ml
$^1/_4$ cup (4 tbsp)	2 fl oz	60 ml
$^1/_3$ cup (5 tbsp)	2$^1/_2$ fl oz	75 ml
$^1/_2$ cup (8 tbsp)	4 fl oz	125 ml
$^2/_3$ cup (10 tbsp)	5 fl oz	150 ml
$^3/_4$ cup (12 tbsp)	6 fl oz	175 ml
1 cup (16 tbsp)	8 fl oz	250 ml
1$^1/_4$ cups	10 fl oz	300 ml
1$^1/_2$ cups	12 fl oz	350 ml
1 pint (2 cups)	16 fl oz	500 ml
2$^1/_2$ cups	20 fl oz (1 pint)	625 ml
5 cups	40 fl oz (1 qt)	1.25 L

Acknowledgments

·········{Thank you!}·········

Creating *On a Stick!* was so much fun but could not have happened without the assistance and guidance of two very important people. First, my partner Adam Pearson, who tirelessly researched and advised on this book and was the willing taste tester during those trips to the state fair. It's his food styling that makes this book the visual treat it is. He is immensely talented with an instinctual way with food, and I'm blessed to work with him every single day of my life. Second, the phenomenal Jenny Park: tester, writer, and assistant food stylist. She's so sharp and wonderful and I consider it an honor to work with her.

This book is dedicated to my friends and food family, the people who have guided me and helped me immeasurably: Kristina Gill, Elise Bauer, Jaden Hair, David Lebovitz, Todd Porter, and Diane Cu—your friendship means the world to me. To Wade and Brittany Hammond and Brooke Burton and especially Gaby Dalkin, thank you. And to Angela and Lori, the best sisters in the world. To my editor Margaret McGuire, designers Jenny Kraemer and Katie Hatz, and the whole team at Quirk: To give me space to be silly is quite serious to me, imagine that! Thank you for your guidance and for making this book so beautiful and fun from cover to cover. A very special token of gratitude goes to Michael Ruhlman, the person who told me to throw caution to the wind and follow my heart and—most important—have fun while doing it.

To Margaret Roach for her guidance, advice, and insight; I thank my lucky stars (and Martha!) for bringing us together. And to the readers of mattbites, every single one of you: I really can't thank you enough for being there. I mean it.

Lastly, thanks to my parents, Ben and Helen Armendariz, for loving me just the way I am.